....

Bride & Groom

....

Wedding Date

BRIDE & GROOM
ENTERTAINING

BRIDE & GROOM ENTERTAINING

AUTHOR
Brigit Légère Binns
GENERAL EDITOR
Chuck Williams

PHOTOGRAPHER
David Matheson

BONNIER BOOKS

Contents

SPECIAL OCCASIONS

About this book

The first years of marriage are an enchanting time. Even couples who have spent years together are now learning new things about each other, as they establish themselves as a new family. What better way to enjoy and nurture the beginning of your lives together than to bring friends and relatives into your embrace, sharing your home and table with them?

We created this book to help young and not-so-young couples navigate the events and occasions for entertaining that they will encounter during these first years and beyond. Whether you want to host a stylish cocktail party to celebrate your first anniversary, put on an elegant brunch to mark a friend's engagement, or take the plunge and invite both of your families to your home for Christmas dinner, this book will guide you each step of the way and help you entertain with confidence and panache.

Chuck Williams

Creating an event

Sometimes, the need for a party presents itself in an obvious way. Perhaps it's almost New Year's Eve and your closest friends haven't yet made dinner reservations. Or, your sister joyfully announces that she is expecting. Or, unbelievably, you and your spouse are nearing an important milestone, your first anniversary.

Other times, the sense of occasion is not as well defined. Indeed, often the best excuse for a party may be that there's nothing to celebrate. You haven't seen your brother for ages, or your friends are all work and no play. Consider this the perfect moment to begin handing out invitations.

Entertaining as a couple can be challenging. Nowadays, when both partners are often accustomed to taking charge in their own work and lives, the give-and-take of marriage can be a new skill to learn. The kitchen can be a metaphor for your larger lives, and there you can practise the fine arts of cooperation, compromise, interacting with grace under pressure, and biting one's tongue when the situation gets a little heated—literally. When the road gets bumpy, remember to appreciate the fact that you have two heads to figure it all out, and four hands to get the work done.

Menu key

This book is divided into three chapters of menus. The first chapter focuses on everyday cocktail and dinner parties. The second chapter moves the party outdoors for alfresco entertaining. And the third chapter features menus for special occasions.

Preparation and cooking times are given at the top of each recipe, and each menu is preceded by a detailed workplan showing exactly when to start preparing each dish in order to have everything ready at the right moment. The workplan also offers wine-pairing suggestions, simple ideas for rounding out a menu, and advice on party setup and style that will help make your event special, down to the last detail.

Planning the event

Now that you've decided to host a party, you will want to give both yourself and your guests time to plan for it. Your party will come off better if you are not rushed when organising it, and your friends will be more likely to be free if they are given ample notice of the date: at least a week for a casual dinner, or two for a more elaborate affair. Special occasions such as holidays deserve even more advance notice, since they may involve travel or gifts.

Before you send out invitations, think about how your event will unfold. A good party "flow" is not a happy accident. The way you arrange your space can encourage the party to take shape the way you want it to. Will a dinner party begin in the living room and move to a formal dining room, or will guests gather in the kitchen? Do you want guests to move from room to room? Ample seating in more than one area, stations with self-service food and drinks, and the movement of the hosts are all ways to keep a party dynamic.

BASIC QUESTIONS

- What time do you want your guests to arrive, and what time do you imagine them leaving?
- As they approach your door, what will they see and who will greet them?
- Where will they put their coats? Do you have enough hangers, or a spare bed where coats can be draped? If there's a chance of rain, where can they place their wet umbrellas?
- Who will offer them a drink and what will that drink be?
- What about an appetizer to go with the drink?
- Do you have enough seating? You can buy a card table to extend your dinner table and borrow or rent chairs, if needed.

Attending to details

Keep your imagination working as your party begins to take shape. As you review the menus in this book, look at the plan that precedes each one to get a sense of how much work it will entail, as well as how much of the work can be done in advance of your party day.

Once you have settled on a party time and menu, continue to run through the event in your mind, filling in details. Think about what little touches would make your guests more comfortable. If you are serving beef satay at a stand-up cocktail party, where can guests dispose of the empty skewers? Can they easily wipe their fingers clean after enjoying your barbequed ribs? If guests set their wineglasses down on a table, how can you help them remember which glass is theirs? If you are planning a meal outdoors, do you have extra sweaters or shawls available in case some guests get cold, or sunscreen for a fair-skinned guest? Do you have tempting nonalcoholic beverages and water to offer as well as wine, beer, and mixed drinks? Anticipating all these concerns is what makes attentive hosts and a memorable party.

SPRING CLEANING

Ideally, you'll give the whole house a thorough cleaning before a party. But if you're pressed for time and can't get everything done, don't worry. Focus your cleaning efforts on the rooms in which guests will be spending the most time and close doors to help direct attention away from areas that you haven't straightened up. Also, airing the house and decorating with fresh flowers and greenery—and with candles if you're planning an evening gathering—will go a long way toward making your space ready for a party.

One place you can't cut corners is the bathroom. Make sure it's spick-and-span, and, more than that, give your guests a pleasant space to freshen up. Stock it with scented soaps, mints, extra tissue paper, a hand mirror, scented candles, and flowers.

Planning the menu

This cookbook offers twelve complete menus, and novice cooks and hosts may want to follow them to the letter, starting with a more casual event and working their way up to a holiday dinner for ten. However, you should always feel free to make changes to the menus, substituting your own ideas once you are comfortable cooking for guests. Just remember to keep a few basic menu-planning rules in mind: incorporate seasonal ingredients; plan a mix of dishes that cook on the stove top or grill and in the oven, to avoid traffic jams; and plan a mix of made-in-advance and last-minute dishes.

Ideally, you'll have a number of dishes or cooking tasks that can be completed well in advance, leaving only a couple of items for last-minute preparation after the party starts. As a married couple, you have two cooks to share the work, but even so, plan things so that you will be able to devote your attention to your guests once they arrive. The more experienced you are at cooking, the more you can leave until the last minute—especially if you don't get stage fright and can invite your guests into the kitchen to talk and sip wine as you cook. With practise, anyone can become comfortable cooking before an audience, but do yourself and your guests a favour and don't try it before you are comfortable. When a host is under stress, no one at the party is having a good time. Bear in mind, too, that a prepared food item or two can make a dinner party menu much easier. If the idea of making every single course in a menu leaves you worried, cut out a dish and substitute something ready-made. This will save you time and energy to devote to your guests instead.

Working as a team

Now that you have selected your menu, the two of you need to plan your time: When do you shop so that all the ingredients are at hand and as fresh as possible? What needs to be done to make your space party-ready and inviting? How far in advance can you start getting dishes ready? Plot everything out on paper, then divide up the tasks in a way that works for you as a couple. You may each prefer to take charge of certain elements of the party and work side-by-side but independently, or one of you may want to take the lead and the other act as helper. Just make sure that the roles are defined and the division of labour is clear, to avoid unnecessary conflict.

SEASONAL COOKING

Always consider seasonality when planning a menu. If you cook with out-of-season ingredients, your food will suffer. Yes, you can find tomatoes in the middle of winter, but they will be bland and cottony in comparison to the juicy, flavourful tomatoes you remember from last summer. Opt instead for dishes that call for season-friendly hard-shelled winter squash or crisp Swiss chard.

TIPS FOR NOVICE HOSTS

- Get organised. The more elaborate the party, the more organised you need to be. Make checklists and timelines. Don't leave the shopping and food preparation until the last minute: do each task as far in advance as it can be done. Consult the menu workplans to see what dishes or chores can be completed ahead of time, and how far ahead.
- Well in advance of the party, make sure you have all the required cooking equipment and serving utensils. Crockery checklists on the menu workplans and tools lists accompanying each recipe will help you determine whether you are prepared.
- Practise makes perfect. Even if you are an experienced cook, don't try out a recipe for the first time on the day of the party. A trial run will make cooking for your guests go more smoothly, and will allow you to make any little adjustments to the menu that you'd like.
- Do yourself a favour and plan your first dinner parties for Saturday nights. This gives you an entire day for last-minute shopping, decorating, and cooking—and another entire day to recover, rest, and clean up! Save weeknight dinner parties for when you feel experienced and confident, or very organised.

Creating a mood

As you think about your party, what kind of a scene comes to mind? Do you imagine a festive, noisy, jubilant evening, or a calm, intimate conversation around the table? A lazy, warm afternoon in the garden, or an evening get-together in the living room? It's up to you to create the atmosphere you want. The type of food you serve is one key to establishing a mood. A hearty braised lamb creates a warm feeling of camaraderie around the table and invites intimate conversation, while the sprightly flavours of spring rolls accompanied with stylish cocktails set the stage for an evening of witty exchanges. Beyond the food, the decorations you choose will set the scene.

BLOSSOMS BLOOMING

The flowers you choose and the way you arrange them will instantly contribute to your party's ambience.

ELEGANT RESTRAINT
Freesias, gerbera daisies, and Iceland poppies are lovely presented as single stems in tall vases or bottles.

DRAMATIC FLAIR
Cherry blossoms, lilies, orchids, pussywillows, sheaves of wheat, and spiky delphiniums or larkspur lend immediate drama to any affair.

GENEROUS DOMES
Use a floral frog and plenty of stems cut short to make gorgeous displays of daffodils, dahlias, hydrangeas, ranunculus, roses and tulips.

SWEET NOSEGAYS
Anemones, chrysanthemums, marigolds, roses and violets are all appealing as small bouquets in metal cups or ceramic pitchers.

FREEFORM FAVORITES
Peonies, snapdragons, cosmos, and sweet peas are charming in simple, loose, unstudied arrangements.

NATURAL BEAUTIES

Bringing the natural world into your space helps to create a pleasant party atmosphere.

The variety of moods that flowers can create is endless: consider the difference between lush, billowing armfuls of blue hydrangeas; tall, graceful, velvety, stark pussywillows rising from a modern urn; the cheerful, eye-popping colours of ranunculus tumbling from an old copper bucket; or a restrained arrangement of unusual green flowers in a simple matte white vase.

Fruits and vegetables, too, offer delightful colors and dramatically represent the seasons: pale green pears and yellow lemons usher in early spring, while fiery orange persimmons and red pomegranates appear only in late fall and winter. Try decorating with these seasonal offerings:

In spring, artichokes, limes, pears, strawberries.

In summer, cherries, purple or ivory aubergines, figs, mangoes, nectarines and peaches, pineapples, yellow squashes, baby courgettes.

In autumn, apples, green and purple artichokes, chillis, dried ears of corn, gourds, grapes, orange and white pumpkins, persimmons.

In winter, lemons, oranges and blood oranges, pears, pomegranates, quinces.

Styling your party

The colours and patterns you use to set off a meal and decorate a room also convey mood. Cool or pale colours, such as periwinkle blue, lavender, platinum, or sea green, create a different feel from warm or rich ones, such as wine red, burnt orange, rose gold, or chocolate brown. Likewise, curvy or floral patterns make a different statement from rules and geometric patterns. Even if you own just one set of white dishes (a versatile choice!), colours and patterns can be brought into your party through table coverings, napkins, flowers and fruit, and serving pieces.

Lighting is yet another way to set a mood. The last thing you want at any party is harsh overhead light. Be kind to your guests and remember that everyone looks good by candlelight. Placing tiny tea candles around a room, floating candles in water-filled crystal bowls, lighting a fire in the fireplace, or setting up tiki torches around the garden patio all inspire a sense of well-being and festivity. And don't forget to light the entrance for an evening party.

COLOUR SCHEMES

You may assume that it's best to decorate with cool colours in summer and warm in winter, but this isn't always true: imagine a Christmas dinner table set with ice blue table linens and sparkling silver. Colour can be used in so many intriguing combinations that it's a shame not to explore a new idea. Paint chips are an interesting (and free!) inspiration. Some ideas:

- dark neutrals with acid colours, like brown with chartreuse, navy with fuchsia
- deep, cool, calm colours mixed with bright, warm ones, such as dark grey with red, or aubergine with orange
- muted, sophisticated monotones such as ecru, periwinkle, or sage green
- jewel tones like emerald, ruby, or sapphire with antique gold, bronze, or pewter

Invitations and place cards

Sending a paper invitation signals a special event and can set the tone for your party. You may decide to carry the style of your invitations over to place cards and drink tags.

- Invitations don't need to be elaborate or expensive—in fact, the most proper and traditional invitation is a handwritten note on plain paper asking a guest to join you.
- Visit an art-supply store for any kind of paper that catches your fancy to make stylish invitations and place cards.
- To make an invitation stand out, roll it up and mail it in a small cardboard canister, available at stationery shops.
- Mail invitations ten days to two weeks before a dinner party to give your guests ample time to reserve the date in their diaries.
- Place cards can be as simple as small pieces of card stock with names written or printed on them, laid at each place setting.
- You can also dispense with the cards altogether and write names on flat stones or on fruits.
- Use a place-card clip or clothes peg for displaying cards, or check a stationery shop for charming, unique clips.
- If you are tying a ribbon around each napkin, use a hole punch to make a hole in the place card and loop the ribbon through it.
- To make drink tags, cut shapes out of card stock or construction paper and, using waxed string, attach them to stems of glasses.

Table coverings and napkin folds

The dressings used on the table, whether a buffet or a dining table, help to set the style of the party. From formal white damask to rustic burlap to jewel-toned dupioni silk, the choices are limited only by your imagination. Napkins, which traditionally sit on the plate at a place setting, can be styled in many ways.

- Layering a table with different types of coverings can create an interesting and unusual effect, especially when you use such contrasting materials and fabrics as silk, linen, leather, and jute. Look for unique beaded, tasselled, embroidered, loosely woven, or quilted runners and place mats to create a unique look.
- Long, narrow runners are usually laid lengthwise down the centre of a table, but using multiple runners crosswise will give the table a fresh look.
- Loosen up the classic rectangular or square napkin fold and hold the ruffled napkin in place with a glass or metal paperweight, a polished river stone, or seasonal fruit.
- Roll up each napkin and tie with ribbon, raffia, a tasseled silk cord, waxed string, or a long slender leaf from the flowers decorating your house or from an ingredient in your menu, such as lemongrass.
- If you have napkin rings in different designs, mix and match them for a cheerful look.
- Visit a local crafts shop, florist, or farmers' market for unique materials that you can use to create your own napkin rings or ornaments.

Centrepieces and lighting

Floral arrangements and candles or other forms of soft lighting can transform your house or garden into a magical setting. Ask the florist about floral foam and flower frogs, which support flower stems inside the vase or bowl and are the secrets to creating dense domes and many other artful arrangements.

- Small bouquets are nice for a dining table, as they don't block the view across the table. Use metal cups or small jugs to repeat an arrangement. Gather flowers into generous clumps, and don't be afraid to cut stems short.
- Make a large bouquet of a particular flower to use as a centrepiece, then place smaller bouquets or a single flower in individual glass vases at guests' place settings or at spots throughout the room.
- Place a single long-stemmed flower in its own tall, narrow vase or bottle to make a simple and graceful statement.
- Wrap tea lights or votives in pieces of tissue or rice paper and secure with twine. Choose paper colours that are contrasting or complementary.
- Fill vases with glass beads, stones, or pebbles to secure tall candlesticks.
- Pair small tea lights or votives with tall candles for a layered lighting effect.
- Arrange multiple column candles in different heights and different shades of the same colour in footed dishes.
- Place a cluster of votives in glass holders on a long, narrow platter or mirror laid on the table.

Aperitifs and food presentation

Within moments of a guest's arrival at your party, offer him or her a refreshment. This gesture is not only courteous, but it buys you time to finish up any last-minute dinner preparations. Below are some marvelously simple suggestions. When serving food on a plate or platter, whether an hors d'oeuvre or a course of a meal, remember to pay attention to the presentation and garnish, making the food visually appealing.

- Offer the French white aperitif wine Lillet Blanc, classically served over ice or with soda and garnished with an orange twist, or the French red aperitif wine Dubonnet Rouge, classically served on its own or mixed with lemonade.
- Mix Campari, an Italian herbal aperitif, with soda or orange juice.
- Simple nibbles that pair well with aperitifs include assorted olive varieties, warmed in olive oil with herbs and lemon zest; gherkins; capers; nuts; quartered figs or melon balls, wrapped with strips of prosciutto; dates; roasted peppers (capsicums) drizzled with olive oil and seasoned with salt and pepper; and *edamame* (salted boiled soybeans in the pod).
- If plating your servings restaurant style, keep portion sizes moderate and arrange the food in an attractive way.
- Use a kitchen towel to wipe spatters from the rim of the plate before it leaves the kitchen.
- Garnish food and cocktails with a sprig of an herb or a slice of citrus used in the recipe, for both colour and a hint of freshness.

Party equipment

Entertaining, like so many other parts of life, is simpler when you have the right tools for the job. The ideas given here are guidelines for what you may find helpful. Be sure to tailor them to your own entertaining style and needs.

When couples get married, a set of crockery is typically among the wedding gifts. You can, of course, make do with just a few basics in the beginning, and build your collection over time. If you're not yet married, and are still trying to decide on what crockery you might like to have, consider plain white porcelain. They go with everything. You can dress them up or down, and you can vary the look of your table with coloured or patterned table linens, serving pieces, and/or chargers. And if you happen to break a plate, you won't have trouble replacing it with one that matches, even years down the road.

PLACE SETTINGS

A traditional five-piece place setting includes a dinner plate, a salad plate, a shallow soup plate (which can double as a pasta bowl), a cup, and a saucer. The basic five-piece cutlery setting includes a dinner knife, a dinner fork, a salad fork, a soupspoon, and a teaspoon.

When registering, estimate the size of the largest dinner party you might host and add a couple of extra settings in case of breakage.

If you plan to entertain often, you'll want a set of bread and butter plates as well as an extra set of salad plates to use for dessert, so that you won't have to wash plates after the main course to use for cake or pie. Likewise, you'll want extra teaspoons and salad forks, so that you will have enough utensils to go from soup to nuts without having to stop and wash dishes.

GLASSES FOR HOPS

Tumblers and highball glasses can be used for beer, although aficionados will want to investigate glasses that show off their favourite beer varieties to best advantage:

Pint glasses: These generous, widemouthed glasses are suitable for any beer, especially a full-bodied ale, bitter, or stout.

Pilsner glasses: These tapered glasses, sometimes designed with a bulge and usually shorter than a pint glass, are designed to show off this pale gold beer and others like it.

Hefeweizen glasses: These tall glasses encourage the billowing head of foam that is a hallmark of the traditional Bavarian wheat beer, prized for its rich, complex flavour with notes of fruit and cloves.

Beer mugs: These sturdy glasses echo the traditional German tankard, or stein.

Glassware

A basic stemware set includes water glasses and wineglasses for reds and whites. The most pared-down choice is the balloon wineglass, which can be used for either white or red wine. The shape of a wineglass, however, affects how the wine tastes and smells, which in turn affects your appreciation of it. If you enjoy exploring wines, you can select additional stemware for specific grape varieties, such as Cabernet, Pinot Noir, or Chardonnay.

If you plan to host cocktail parties, be sure your glassware selections include items like highballs, double old-fashioneds, and stemmed martini, or cocktail, glasses, as well as bar tools and accessories.

Register for at least twice as many wineglasses as dinnerware place settings to ensure you have enough glasses for the cocktail hour and for dinner, and to cover breakage (which, of course, is more of a problem with glasses than with plates). Choose sturdy, versatile glassware for everyday use and casual entertaining.

GLASSES FOR GRAPES

Cabernet glasses: For intense, high-tannin red wines of medium acidity, such as Cabernet, Bordeaux, Cabernet Franc, Merlot.

Pinot glasses: For medium-bodied red wines of high acidity, such as Pinot Noir, Burgundy, Barbera, Barolo, Nebbiolo.

Syrah glasses: For fruity, rich red wines, such as Syrah (Shiraz), Barbera, Châteauneuf-du-Pape, Hermitage Rouge, Malbec, Zinfandel.

Chardonnay glasses: For medium- to full-bodied dry white wines, such as Chardonnay, Chablis, Chenin Blanc, Pinot Grigio, Viognier.

Sauvignon Blanc glasses: For light-bodied white wines ranging from high acidity to off-dry, such as Sauvignon Blanc, Sancerre, Gewürztraminer, Riesling, Sémillon.

Linens

A simple white tablecloth is a handy item to have on hand in your linen cupboard, as it is suitable for any occasion and complements most table settings. But think of linens as an expressive way to change the look of your table from season to season, or to dress up your table for special occasions. It's a good idea to have a stock of extra tablecloths, place mats, and napkins in case of stains.

Serveware

Over time, you will want to acquire enough serveware to accommodate family-style brunches, buffets, formal sit-down dinners, and everything in between.

Neutral-coloured serving pieces are the most flexible, since they coordinate beautifully with most dinnerware and table settings. Consider decorative serveware, such as plain or hand-painted ceramic platters, bowls, and jugs, to give your table flair. These pieces can help create a memorable mood at a party. On pages 22–23 you will find lists of items you'll want for specific types of entertaining. Each list builds on the next one.

CASUAL DINNER PARTIES

- napkins and place mats
- wine opener
- tumblers for wine, beer, and water, or balloon wineglasses for wine
- salad plates
- soup or pasta bowls
- dinner plates
- dessert plates or bowls
- salad forks, dinner forks, soupspoons, knives, teaspoons, dessert forks
- water jug
- wooden salad bowl and salad servers
- serving bowls and platters
- serving spoons and forks
- coffee pot
- teapot
- coffee mugs
- milk jug and sugar bowl

COCKTAIL PARTIES

- old-fashioned glasses
- highball glasses
- martini glasses
- Tom Collins glasses
- white and red wineglasses
- pilsner glasses or beer mugs
- margarita glasses
- cocktail shaker with strainer
- glass jug and long spoon
- bar tools set
- ice bucket and tongs
- wine and champagne buckets
- wooden muddler
- cocktail picks for garnishes
- cocktail napkins
- appetizer plates

FORMAL DINNER PARTIES

- tablecloths
- table runners
- formal napkins
- napkin rings
- chargers
- white and red wineglasses or grape variety–specific glasses
- decanter
- water goblets
- bread basket
- butter dish
- bread and butter plates
- individual butter knives
- hostess sets: serving spoon, serving fork, gravy ladle, and pastry server
- cheese board
- cheese knives
- cordial glasses
- brandy glasses
- cups and saucers and/or espresso cups and saucers

HOLIDAY ENTERTAINING

- champagne flutes
- additional bread basket
- additional butter dish
- gravyboat
- turkey platter
- carving board
- carving set
- soup tureen
- casserole dish
- cake or tart stand

Party settings

The arrangement of plates, glasses, and cutlery for a place setting may seem arcane and difficult to remember if you don't understand the concept behind it, which is actually quite simple: everything is placed in order of use and within easy reach.

Casual table setting

Whether a meal is casual or formal in style, each utensil at a place setting should have its use and be placed where the diner will find it most quickly and easily. (See details on proper placement at right). Even for a casual setting, attention to detail shines through.

Decide whether you will use a tablecloth, runner(s), place mats, or some other form of table dressing. For each place setting, lay down the plate, allowing plenty of room between diners. Fold a napkin and place it on the plate, or to the left of the plate beneath the fork.

Set a water glass directly above the knife. For a casual dinner, a simple balloon wineglass may be used for either red or white. Align the bottom of the cutlery with the bottom rim of the dinner plate.

Don't worry about placing dessert utensils on the table. When it's time for dessert and coffee, clear away everything except the water glass and bring in the utensils with dessert.

Formal table setting

The formal table setting is more elaborate than a casual one, but does not differ in essentials. Each plate, glass, and utensil is positioned to help the diner enjoy his or her meal with ease.

If desired, place a charger beneath the dinner plate to add interest. Place the napkin on the plate. The salad or soup plate goes on top of the dinner plate and should be removed after the first course.

If you're using a bread plate, position it above the forks, with an individual butter knife laid across it. You can set dessert utensils above the plate (fork handle pointing left, teaspoon handle pointing right) or bring them in with dessert.

RULES OF ORDER

Cutlery is arranged by order of use from the outside in:

- Forks are set to the left of the plate. Whether you eat American style (fork in left hand for cutting, right hand for eating) or European style (fork in left hand at all times), this is where you will first instinctively reach for a fork when you commence a meal.
- Knives are set to the right of the plate with blade facing the plate, again to help the diner make use of it in the most natural way.
- Spoons are set to the outside of the knife when the meal begins with a soup course.
- First-course salad forks are set to the outside of dinner forks.

Glasses sit above the knife, where a diner naturally reaches for a drink with his right hand. Wineglasses sit to the right of water glasses, in the order in which they will be served.

A PARADE OF GLASSES

When setting a formal table, you may have multiple wineglasses to contend with. Here are the traditional positions for all glasses:

- Place the water goblet about 5 cm (2 in) above the dinner knife.
- If multiple wines will be served, their respective glasses sit to the right of the water glass in the order they will be used (usually white, then red, or lighter-bodied ones before fuller-bodied ones).
- The wineglasses can be lined up in a row that extends diagonally to the right, lined up in a row parallel to the edge of the table, or grouped into a triangle.
- Bring in dessert wineglasses with dessert.

Buffet service

If you plan to serve a meal buffet style, you will need a sideboard or table to serve the food from. Check in advance that what you choose is large enough for the menu you are planning. Get out all the serving pieces you will need to present the meal, label each one with the dish it will hold, and arrange them on the table.

You can push together two or three tables and cover them with a tablecloth to make a surface large enough for a buffet. If you're setting up a large buffet on a round table, position the table away from the wall so that guests can circulate around it.

Each serving platter or bowl should be paired with the proper serving utensils. Make sure the serving pieces are not so close together that guests will jostle one another as they serve themselves.

When you are planning a brunch buffet, you can arrange all of the serveware on the buffet the night before and leave it in place to save preparation time in the morning.

Cocktail-bar setup

The ritual and ceremony involved in cocktail construction are probably as much fun as drinking the cocktail itself, and the bar area (along with the kitchen) is where guests are most likely to congregate. So, take some time to carefully plan the space.

If you don't have a stand-alone or built-in bar, you can create a temporary or permanent one using a cabinet, bookshelf, trolley, or side table. Since guests will be milling around the bar, try to pick a spot—perhaps an inviting corner in the kitchen, dining room, or living room—that won't interfere with the flow of traffic throughout the rooms.

Stocking the bar may seem overwhelming (and rather expensive) unless you buy supplies incrementally, tailored to your favourite drinks and the preferences of particularly good friends. Use the list at right as a starting point and gradually fill it in with your own preferred spirits, liqueurs, wines, and beers. Always keep plenty of soda and sparkling fruit juices on hand for teetotalers, as well as garnishes. And don't forget to keep a book of cocktail recipes stashed behind the bar for any unfamiliar requests.

DIRECTING TRAFFIC

To arrange a buffet table, decide in which direction guests will move along it to serve themselves, and arrange the serving pieces in this order. Place the plates at the beginning point of the buffet, and place napkins and cutlery at the other end. These can be laid out on a tray, or the cutlery may be bundled in napkins and tied. You can also bundle cutlery and napkins in a place mat and tie with a length of ribbon or raffia.

If you have a mix of hot and cold foods, have guests help themselves to the cold foods first, and work their way to the hot ones. That way, the hot foods won't cool off too much while they are serving themselves the cold dishes.

It's difficult to fill up a plate with a glass in one hand, so set up a separate beverage buffet away from the food buffet, or place the glasses at the end of the buffet with the utensils.

THE BASIC BAR

- VODKA
- GIN
- SILVER TEQUILA
- RUM, LIGHT AND DARK
- SCOTCH WHISKY
- BOURBON
- DRY (WHITE) VERMOUTH
- ANGOSTURA BITTERS
- TRIPLE SEC, GRAND MARNIER, OR COINTREAU
- SWEET (RED) VERMOUTH
- BRANDY AND/OR COGNAC
- SODA, TONIC, AND GINGER ALE; FRUIT JUICES

PARTIES

There are many occasions that call for a party, from a promotion at work to a friend's visit from out of town. But remember, you don't need any reason to host a party beyond a desire to do something nice for friends and family.

The all-purpose parties in this chapter can be dressed up or down. You make the call, with your choice of decorations and flowers, and the look of the glasses and dishware. The Classic Cocktail Party, for example, can be made into a stylish affair, with vintage martini glasses and streamlined divided dishes for the hors d'oeuvres, or it can be transformed into a savoury spread for a casual gathering focused on a televised sporting event. The formality and tone of a party is indicated by the relative formality of the invitation. An e-mailed invitation or one extended by telephone usually signals an informal event, while printed or hand-lettered paper invitations signal a more formal atmosphere (and possibly even a dress code!).

HOW MUCH WILL THEY EAT AND DRINK?

In general, a cocktail party that takes place at the dinner hour should provide guests with enough food to replace a meal, while an early-evening get-together should offer just a few delicious bites, with the understanding that guests will be going on to dinner elsewhere.

Plan on serving three drinks per every two hours for each guest. This may seem like a lot, but it is better to have extra on hand than to come up short.

As responsible hosts, you will want to provide your guests with sufficient food and water to prevent drunkenness, encourage guests to designate a driver who will remain sober, and be sure to provide plenty of hot coffee with all the fixings as the evening winds down.

SHAKEN OR STIRRED?

We know James Bond's opinion on the subject, but how many of us understand the question?

The primary goal of both shaking and stirring is to chill a "neat" cocktail by putting the liquid in direct contact with ice. Shaking is a more effective method of chilling, and a thorough chilling is essential in a good cocktail. However, shaking also causes ice to melt more quickly, watering down a cocktail slightly, even when the ice is quickly strained out. This may or may not be a concern.

Because shaking creates cloudiness and bubbles, stirring is a good choice for cocktails made from clear spirits that benefit from a crystal-clear appearance. So, despite Bond's preference, stirring is a good way to prepare a martini. And the concern you sometimes hear about "bruising the gin"? Never fear. It probably originated as a witty remark.

Hosting a cocktail party

A cocktail party is distinguished from a dinner party not only by the style and quantity of the food served, but also because it is typically a stand-up, rather than a sit-down, occasion. That distinction makes it a good idea to separate the cocktail bar from the hors d'oeuvre buffet, so that guests will flow from one to the other, meeting an old or a new friend along the way. You could place the bar and buffet at either end of a large room, or even put them in separate rooms.

A cocktail party can be formal, informal, or a relaxed combination of the two. A combination of passed foods with a buffet makes for a warm atmosphere, and is the kind of event that is perfect for a two-host party. One host can circulate with a platter, encouraging easy conversation and mingling among the guests, while the other checks the buffet for used napkins and glasses and almost-empty platters. For a more formal party, forgo the buffet and enlist or hire an extra pair of hands, passing all the foods on platters. You may also want to pass cocktails on light but sturdy trays, for an elegant effect.

Attending to details

Be sure to anticipate your guests' needs by having on hand plenty of bottled water and soda; appealing garnishes such as fresh limes, mint sprigs, and maraschino cherries; and lots of clean glasses. Consider guests who won't be drinking alcohol and mix up a special beverage such as mint iced tea or homemade lemonade.

For a themed cocktail party, you might decide to limit the beverages to those on your menu, or you can provide a limited backup bar as well, offering standard spirits like vodka, whisky, bourbon, and gin, as well as mixers such as fruit juices, soda water, and tonic. Assign a bartender—one of you two, a friend, or, for a special occasion, a professional—who will create cocktails to order. Or, require some little degree of self-service from your guests. You can set a table attractively with ice buckets, bottles, and garnishes for guests to help themselves—or perhaps take it a step further, and put out cocktail ingredients along with simple drink recipes printed on cards. Another alternative is to mix a cocktail or two in quantity and set them out in nice jugs. This will free you up to mingle, while still ensuring that your guests are well taken care of.

PRODUCE OF FRANCE
BOTTLED IN FRANCE
Triple Orange
Grand Marnier
Maison fondée en 1827
750 ml
LIQUEUR
PARIS - FRANCE
LIQUEUR

Hosting a dinner party

At dinner parties, guests expect to sit down at a table with a place setting, rather than circulate with a plate, as at an informal buffet. With that in mind, planning the guest list for a dinner party becomes more important than it might be for other types of party. First, decide how many people you would like to have. If you have a small home, a small table, a limited number of matching place settings, or limited time to prepare, you will want to keep the guest list shorter. Then consider the mingling of guests: Would you like to introduce people who have never met? If so, do they have similar interests that will likely lead to enjoyable exchanges, or are you and your spouse adept at encouraging conversation? On the other hand, would you like to keep the party limited to friends who know one another? This might be a birthday celebration or a reunion of college friends. Just because everyone knows one another well is no reason not to put your best foot forward with the menu and decorations.

Attending to details

Once you have put together the guest list, it's time to plan the menu and conceive a mood or theme that you can carry throughout the space. The season can inform not only the dishes you serve, but also your choice of decorations and colours for the table, from flowers and fruit to linens to party favours. With the basics of theme and colour decided, look for other ways to enhance the chosen mood, using candles, music, or even serving method, opting for either plating the meal restaurant style in the kitchen or passing platters of food family style at the dining table.

More important than the food or decorations is the attention that you direct toward your guests. From the moment they arrive, your role is to make them feel that they are welcome and will be well cared for. Be prepared to offer them a drink and something to eat immediately, even if a formal sit-down dinner is planned. You can stage such offerings in any comfortable seating area, or you can set up a table in the kitchen where everyone will gather. If you think it will add interest to start in one room and then move to another, have both spaces prepared and be ready to cue your guests when it's time to move, so that the party doesn't lose its shape or conviviality but instead flows naturally from one setting to the next.

THE SEATING CHART

To help ensure a successful dinner party, plan the seating arrangements. Time-honoured traditions include alternating men and women around the table and not seating spouses together. Both conventions lead to more interesting conversations.

It's also traditional to put a female guest of honour to the right of the male host, and a male guest of honour to the right of the female host. This guarantees that respected guests receive attention throughout the dinner.

If you are introducing guests to one another, plan your seating based on shared interests or another likely basis for conversation.

Once you have worked out the best seating arrangement, signal your intentions with place cards. The design of your place cards is limited only by your imagination; see page 16 for a few ideas to get you started.

ROUNDING OUT A MEAL

To supplement a menu with a few nice extras, offer olives, almonds, or flavoured rice crackers with the pre-dinner aperitifs, which might be wine or a traditional, mild European cocktail such as Dubonnet and soda.

Another luxurious addition: Offer a cheese course, before or in lieu of dessert. Select one mild, one blue, and one aged cheese and place them on a cheese board, accompanied by crackers or baguette slices, cheese knives, and fruit, such as bunches of grapes, dates, or figs. You might use cards to identify each cheese, its type of milk, and its country of origin. If all your cheeses come from one country, select a dessert wine or digestif to match, such as Sauternes with French cheeses, or *vin santo* for an Italian selection.

Classic cocktail party

Host a fifties-fabulous affair featuring all the classic retro offerings, from a gin martini (shaken or stirred) to hot crab dip with crostini and prawn kebabs with a little bit of kick.

Old-Fashioned Cocktail

Classic Martini

Manhattan Cocktail

Retro Relish Tray

Crab Dip with Crostini

Cayenne and Garlic Prawns

Stuffed Cherry Tomatoes

SERVES 8–10

Well in advance of the party, practise making the cocktails until you're able to craft each one while holding a conversation. Alternatively, enlist a friend to tend bar.

Ahead of time

General party prep

Week of the party

- Assemble the necessary serving pieces:
  - *8–10 martini or old-fashioned glasses*
  - *Divided-compartment dish(es) for relish tray*
  - *Baking or soufflé dish and heatproof platter for dip*
  - *Platter(s) for prawns*
  - *Large plate or platter for stuffed tomatoes*
- Plan to set up separate stations for cocktails and hors d'oeuvres in different rooms, to encourage guests to circulate. The hors d'oeuvre station should include small plates and napkins, and a place to dispose of skewers.
- Select music for party. Try classic crooners: Frank Sinatra, Tony Bennett, Serge Gainsbourg.
- Plan decorations with flowers and candles.
- Clean the house.

Food and drink

Week of the party

- Visit a good off licence to stock up on gin, vodka, whisky, bourbon, and other bar needs.
- Practise making each cocktail until you're able to craft each one while holding a conversation.

Up to 1 day ahead

- Make a list and go grocery shopping.
- Make crostini and assemble crab dip.
- Make garlic butter.

The night before the party

- Resist temptation to eat crab dip.

	Day of the party	After the party starts
	Early in the day ■ Decorate the house. ■ Assemble the cocktail-bar equipment and glasses. ■ Ready coffee service in the kitchen so that it's easy to begin brewing a pot as the evening winds down. **1 hour ahead** ■ Stock up on ice. Store extra bags of ice in a bath, ice chest, or large tub covered with layers of newspaper, a great insulator. **Just before the party starts** ■ Set out garnishes at the bar and fill ice buckets.	**During the party** ■ While one host mans the bar, the other can move from group to group and offer one of the finger foods from a tray (and keep an eye on the hors d'oeuvre buffet to make sure it is stocked and tidy). **1 hour after official party start time** ■ Bartender restocks bar with ice from the tub or chest.
	Up to 2 hours ahead ■ Assemble relish tray ingredients, cover, and chill. ■ Soak skewers; thread prawns onto skewers and refrigerate. ■ Make blue cheese filling and hollow tomatoes. **Up to ½ hour ahead** ■ Put out relish tray. ■ Stuff cherry tomatoes. ■ Make lemon twists for cocktails. **Just before the party starts** ■ Put crab dip in oven.	**As soon as guests arrive** ■ Start mixing cocktails. ■ Put prawns under grill.

Old-Fashioned Cocktail

mixing **1** minute | **1** serving

Muddling *is a common term in the world of mixology. It means to gently bruise fruits, herbs, or other ingredients against the base of the glass to release flavours and aromas.*

tools | old-fashioned glass | muddler | jigger | cocktail stirrer

3 dashes Angostura bitters

1 orange slice

1 lemon wedge

1 maraschino cherry

1 sugar cube

Ice cubes

1 jigger plus 1 pony (70 ml /2½ fl oz) blended Canadian whisky **(see page 185)**

In an old-fashioned glass, combine the bitters, orange slice, lemon wedge, cherry, and sugar cube. Muddle the ingredients by mashing them firmly against the base of the glass with a wooden muddler.

Fill the glass with ice, add the whisky, and stir well. Serve immediately.

muddling A muddler, which looks like a miniature baseball bat, is a bartender's tool, used for crushing fruit and herbs to release flavours and aromas. If you don't have one, use the handle of a wooden spoon.

Classic Martini

chilling glasses **1** hour | mixing **1** minute | **1** serving

There are as many variations on the classic martini as there are flavours of vodka. This standard version, however, has stood the test of time. Purists will choose gin, but vodka is a deservedly popular variation. To make a "dry" martini, use less vermouth. Indeed, experiment with the proportions to create your own perfect martini.

tools | channel knife | martini glass | cocktail shaker | jigger

Ice cubes

2 jiggers (90 ml /3 fl oz) gin or vodka

1–2 tsp dry vermouth

Pimiento-stuffed green olive or lemon twist (below) for garnish

For an "up" cocktail, chill a martini glass in the freezer. Or, to serve "on the rocks," fill an old-fashioned glass with ice.

Fill a cocktail shaker half full with ice. Add the gin and the vermouth to taste. Cover with the lid and shake vigorously for 10–20 seconds, then strain into the prepared glass. Garnish with the olive or lemon twist and serve immediately.

a martini with a twist To make a lemon twist, use a channel knife (or the large notch on a citrus zester). This tool will help you peel off the peel in such a way that it curls prettily. For best flavour, cut the twist over the glass, or at least twist it over the glass to release the essential oils. For a lemon martini, substitute lemon-flavoured vodka for the gin and garnish with the lemon twist. Or, try other flavoured vodkas for myriad variations.

Manhattan Cocktail

chilling glasses **1** hour | mixing **1** minute | **1** serving

The origins of famous cocktails are often disputed, but it's widely agreed that the Manhattan was named after a club of the same name and was invented at a party thrown there by Winston Churchill's mother, Jenny.

tools | martini glass | cocktail shaker | jigger

Ice cubes

1 jigger plus 1 pony (70 ml /2½ fl oz) bourbon or rye whiskey

1½ Tbsp sweet vermouth

2 dashes of Angostura bitters

1 maraschino cherry

For an "up" cocktail, chill a martini glass in the freezer. Or, to serve "on the rocks," fill an old-fashioned glass with ice.

Fill a cocktail shaker half full with ice. Add the whiskey, vermouth, and bitters. Cover with the lid and shake vigorously for 10–20 seconds, then strain into the prepared glass. Top with the cherry and serve immediately.

Retro Relish Tray

preparation **15** minutes | chilling **1½** hours | **8–10** cocktail-party servings

This assembly of cold, crunchy, salty, and sweet items—served plain, with no dressing or dip—makes a perfect complement to cocktails. Serve in harmonious small serving bowls or, ideally, in the spirit of the original, a divided-compartment dish made just for this kind of relish selection. Be sure to chill thoroughly in advance.

tools | paring knife | chef's knife | colander

3 bunches radishes

2 heads celery

1 jar (280 g /9 oz) capers, well drained

1 jar (375 g /12 oz) cornichons or gherkins

750 g (24 oz) mixed olives

1 jar (250 g /8 oz) pickled watermelon rind or cocktail onions, well drained

Ice, as needed

Trim the radishes and, if desired, halve lengthwise. Rinse and pat dry, and place in a serving bowl. Remove the large, stringier outer stalks from the celery heads until you reach the pale green heart; reserve the outer stalks for another use. Trim the stem end off the heart and discard. Separate into stalks, rinse thoroughly, and pat dry. Cut the stalks into 4-cm-by-12-mm (1½-by-½-in) pieces.

Arrange the trimmed radishes, celery sticks, capers, gherkins, olives, and watermelon rind in separate serving bowls, or divide them among the compartments of a relish serving dish. Refrigerate all the ingredients, covered with cling film, until well chilled, 1½ hours. If desired, the radishes and celery may be held in ice water until just before serving to give them extra crispness.

When you're ready to serve, if desired, nestle the bowl of radishes in a larger bowl of crushed ice. Serve the tray, keeping any extras refrigerated until ready to refill.

Crab Dip with Crostini

preparation **20** minutes | cooking **35** minutes | **8–10** cocktail-party servings (about 24 bites)

This retro and restorative hot-and-cheesy dip is reminiscent of suburban lawn parties of the fifties. Just the thing to munch with a strong, classic cocktail, it can be assembled in advance and baked just before serving, making it an ideal dish for all kinds of parties.

tools | box grater | serrated bread knife | brush (optional) | baking sheet | large mixing bowl | small baking dish

FOR THE CROSTINI

24 slices baguette, 6mm (¼ in) thick (about 1 large baguette)

Olive oil spray or olive oil for brushing

FOR THE CRAB DIP

250 ml (8 fl oz) mayonnaise

125 g (4 oz) grated Cheddar cheese

250 g (8 oz) cream cheese, softened

1½ tsp Old Bay seasoning, plus more for dusting

1 tsp Worcestershire sauce

½ tsp fine sea salt

¼ tsp ground white pepper

¼ tsp dry mustard

500 g (1 lb) fresh-cooked lump or backfin crabmeat, picked over for shell pieces and cartilage

To make the crostini, preheat the oven to 180°C (350°F). Arrange the baguette slices on a baking sheet and spray or brush them lightly on both sides with the olive oil. Bake until golden, 10–15 minutes. *At this point, the crostini can be stored in an airtight container at room temperature for up to 1 day.*

To make the crab dip, in a large bowl, combine the mayonnaise, 90 g (3 oz) of the Cheddar cheese, the cream cheese, Old Bay seasoning, Worcestershire sauce, salt, pepper, and dry mustard. Beat with a fork until smooth. Fold in the crabmeat, taking care not to break it up too much. Spoon the mixture into a small baking dish or soufflé dish and sprinkle with the remaining 35 g (1 oz) Cheddar. *At this point, the crab dip can be covered and refrigerated for up to 1 day before baking.*

If the oven is not still on from baking the crostini, preheat it to 180°C (350°F). Dust the crab mixture with a little more Old Bay seasoning. Bake until golden on top and bubbling around the edges, 15–20 minutes.

Place the hot crab dip in the centre of a large, heatproof serving platter and arrange the crostini around the dip. Serve at once.

Cayenne and Garlic Prawns

preparation **25** minutes | cooking **10** minutes | **8–10** cocktail-party servings (35 skewers)

These prawns have a subtle bite of spice and garlic. Shelled to make them easy to eat, they are sure to become a snack frequently requested by your lucky guests.

tools | paring knife | garlic press | 35 small skewers | 2 baking sheets | small saucepan | brush

1.75 kg (3½ lb) large prawns, peeled, with tail segments intact, and deveined

Vegetable oil for preparing pans

125 g (4 oz) unsalted butter

4 large cloves garlic, crushed through a press

½ tsp fine sea salt

¼ tsp freshly ground black pepper

¼ tsp ground cayenne pepper

Soak 35 small bamboo skewers in water for 30 minutes. Drain and thread 2 prawns onto each skewer, curling each prawn up and inserting the skewer so it passes through the prawn twice. *At this point, the kebabs can be refrigerated for up to 2 hours.*

Preheat the grill and position the rack 10 cm (4 in) from the heat source. Line 2 large rimmed baking sheets with foil, oil the foil, and arrange the assembled kebabs on the sheets.

In a small saucepan over medium-low heat, combine all of the remaining ingredients and cook, stirring, until the butter is melted. Remove from the heat. Brush the prawns on both sides with the butter, reserving some for basting.

Slide the first pan under the grill and grill for 2 minutes, then slide the pan out and baste the tops of the prawns with half of the reserved butter mixture (do not turn them over). Grill until pink, firm, and slightly golden, 2–3 minutes longer. Transfer

Stuffed Cherry Tomatoes

preparation **25** minutes | **8–10** cocktail-party servings (40 bites)

These little bites of refreshing tomato and savoury cheese are so easy to pop into your mouth while chatting, you may want to double the recipe.

tools | chef's knife | serrated utility knife | food processor | melon baller

125 g (¼ lb) blue cheese, softened

90 g (3 oz) cream cheese, softened

2 Tbsp sour cream

20 cherry tomatoes, halved through the stem end

Sliced spring onions for garnish

Combine the blue cheese, cream cheese, and sour cream in a food processor. Process until smooth, scraping down the sides of the work bowl as needed.

Using the smaller end of a melon baller or a teaspoon, carefully scoop out the seeds and central rib from each tomato half. Arrange cut side up on a plate. *At this point, the tomatoes and cheese mixture can be refrigerated for up to 2 hours.*

About 20 minutes before serving, using 2 small spoons, stuff about ¾ tsp of the blue cheese mixture into each tomato half, mounding it up over the rim. Garnish with spring onions, arrange on a platter, and serve.

Sake party

This menu celebrates the bright, aromatic flavours of Southeast Asia, from a cool cucumber cocktail to citrusy lemongrass beef to savoury spring onion pancakes with soy dipping sauce.

Ginger Cocktail

Cucumber Cooler

Sesame Cucumber Salad

Lemongrass Beef Satay

Spring Onion Pancakes

SERVES 8–10

This party features two easy and refreshing signature cocktails. Instead of making each cocktail to order, mix up batches in advance for guests to pour for themselves.

Ahead of time

General party prep

Week of the party

- Assemble the necessary serving pieces:
  - *2 or more jugs for cocktails*
  - *Small jugs for cucumber purée and simple syrup*
  - *Small platters for cocktail garnishes*
  - *8–10 highball glasses and 8–10 martini glasses*
  - *Serving bowl for cucumber salad*
  - *Platters for satay and pancakes*
  - *A small serving bowl for dipping sauce*
  - *8–10 sets chopsticks (disposable ones, if desired)*
- Plan decorations with flowers and candles.
- Clean the house.

Food and drink

Up to 2 months ahead

- Make and refrigerate simple syrup.

Week of the party

- Visit a good off licence to stock up on sake and other bar needs.

Up to 2 days ahead

- Make a list and go grocery shopping.
- Make peanut dipping sauce for beef.

Up to 1 day ahead

- Make and refrigerate cucumber salad.
- Cook spring onions for pancakes.
- Make dipping sauce for pancakes.

Day of the party	After the party starts
Early in the day ■ Decorate the house. ■ Set up a cocktail bar and a food buffet, complete with receptacles for skewer and/or chopstick disposal.	**During the party** ■ Screen the 1960s classic *The World of Suzie Wong,* with the volume off, on a television in the den or kitchen.
Up to 6 hours ahead ■ Make cucumber purée for cocktails. ■ Grate ginger. **Up to 4 hours ahead** ■ Cube and marinate beef. **Up to 1 hour ahead** ■ Soak and assemble skewers. **Up to ½ hour ahead** ■ Mix cocktails in jugs, if desired. ■ Grill beef kebabs. ■ Make pancake batter. **Just before the party starts** ■ Cook pancakes.	**As guests arrive** ■ Stir and pour cocktails from jugs, or mix individual cocktails. **During the party** ■ Make cocktails as needed and circulate platters of food, alternating the jobs with your spouse. ■ Offer bowls of wasabi peas and crisp, multicoloured rice crackers to round out the menu. ■ Finish the evening with hot green tea, mochi ice-cream morsels, and crystallised ginger.

Ginger Cocktail

chilling glasses **1** hour | preparation **10** minutes | mixing **1** minute | **1** serving

This cocktail has an unexpected punch, one that is warmly welcomed by fans of spicy, full-flavoured concoctions and is sure to surprise everyone.

tools | vegetable peeler | ginger grater | martini glass | chef's knife | cocktail shaker | jigger

1 knob fresh ginger, plus crystallised ginger strips for garnish

1–2 sprigs fresh mint

Ice cubes

1 jigger (45 ml /1½ fl oz) vodka

½ pony (1 Tbsp /15 ml /½ fl oz) sake

½ tsp simple syrup (page 176)

Lime wedge

Peel the fresh ginger with a vegetable peeler and grate it on a ginger grater or the finest rasps of a box grater. Measure out 1½ tsp for 1 cocktail, or to taste. *At this point, the ginger can be refrigerated for up to 6 hours.*

Chill a martini glass in the freezer. Chop the mint finely and measure out ½ tsp. Fill a cocktail shaker three-quarters full with ice. Add the vodka, sake, simple syrup, grated ginger, and chopped mint. Cover with the lid and shake vigorously for 10–20 seconds, then strain into the prepared glass. Squeeze the lime wedge into the cocktail, discarding the lime. Garnish with crystallised ginger.

Cucumber Cooler

preparation **20** minutes | cooling **30** minutes | mixing **1** minute | **1** serving

This sake cocktail is cool, light, refreshing, and pretty to look at. Choose a medium-quality sake: The delicate perfume of a superpremium sake would be lost in a mixed drink. If you are clever with your hands, serve the cooler in a hollowed-out piece of cucumber with a cucumber swizzle stick.

tools | saucepan | citrus reamer | chef's knife | small metal spoon | blender | highball glass | jigger | cocktail stirrer

2 jiggers (90 ml /3 fl oz) sake

2 Tbsp simple syrup (page 176)

1 pony (30 ml /1 fl oz) fresh lime juice, plus 1 small lime wedge for garnish

1 Tbsp fresh cucumber purée (right)

Ice cubes

Club soda for topping

In a highball glass, combine the sake, simple syrup, lime juice, and cucumber purée. Fill the glass with ice and stir to mix well. Top to the rim with club soda. Garnish with the lime wedge and serve immediately.

cucumber purée Peel a cucumber, cut it in half lengthwise, and scrape out the seeds with the tip of a metal spoon. Cut into chunks, place in a blender or food processor, and purée until smooth. One standard cucumber will yield about 250 ml (8 fl oz) purée. You can make the cucumber purée up to 6 hours ahead. Cover and refrigerate.

Sesame Cucumber Salad

preparation **20** minutes | standing **30** minutes | chilling **2** hours | **8–10** cocktail-party servings

Don't skimp on the chilling time for this pretty green salad: part of its charm comes from the cool, juicy texture of the softened cucumber.

tools | chef's knife | vegetable peeler | small metal spoon | mixing bowl | colander

Peel the cucumbers, leaving a few strips of peel if unwaxed. Cut them in half lengthwise, and scrape out any seeds with the tip of a spoon. Slice thinly crosswise. Combine the cucumbers, salt, and sugar in a large bowl. Toss to distribute the sugar and salt evenly, and let stand for 30 minutes. Transfer to a colander; rinse and drain well, then squeeze out excess moisture with your hands (the cucumbers will have become soft and pliable but will still be bright green).

In a serving bowl, stir together the vinegar, garlic, chilli flakes, and sesame seeds. Add the cucumbers and toss to coat. Thinly slice the spring onions and sprinkle them over the top. Cover and refrigerate until well chilled, about 2 hours. *At this point, the salad can be refrigerated for up to 1 day before serving.* Serve cold.

4 cucumbers

1½ Tbsp sea salt

1 Tbsp sugar

125 ml (4 fl oz) unseasoned rice vinegar

3 cloves garlic, chopped

Scant 1 tsp red chilli flakes

1 Tbsp sesame seeds

6 spring onions

Lemongrass Beef Satay

preparation **20** minutes | marinating **2** hours | cooking **10** minutes | **8–10** cocktail-party servings (30 skewers)

This satay is perfect cocktail-party fare: it's easy to eat with one hand, will satisfy the meat lovers in the crowd, and will tame the hunger of after-work party guests.

tools | chef's knife | vegetable peeler | wooden spoon | mixing bowl | 30 skewers | tongs

Cut the beef into small cubes. Combine the lemongrass, ginger, garlic, sesame oil, honey, ½ tsp salt, and ¼ tsp pepper to make a paste. Add the beef and toss to coat, then cover and refrigerate for 2–4 hours. Soak the skewers for 30 minutes.

Preheat the grill and place the rack about 10 cm (4 in) from the heat source. Drain the skewers. Divide the beef among the skewers, pushing the cubes fairly tightly together to prevent them from drying out. Place the assembled skewers on the grill pan and grill, turning every 2 minutes with tongs, for 8–10 minutes total. Meanwhile, stack the lettuce leaves and finely slice them crosswise. Make a bed of the shredded lettuce on a serving platter.

Transfer the satay to the platter. *At this point, the satay can be held for about 15 minutes before serving.* Serve with the dipping sauce.

1.5 kg (3 lb) boneless sirloin steak

3 Tbsp *each* minced fresh lemongrass, peeled and minced ginger, and minced garlic

2 tsp Asian sesame oil

1 Tbsp honey

Sea salt and ground pepper

Lettuce leaves for serving

Peanut dipping sauce (page 125)

Spring Onion Pancakes

preparation **30** minutes | cooking **6** minutes per batch | **8–10** cocktail-party servings

Every good (and responsible) cocktail-party menu includes a starch dish, and these green pancakes fill the role while providing an intriguing taste of spicy Asian flavours. The pancakes are small, so arrange them overlapping on a platter and instruct guests to fold them in half for dipping in the sauce.

tools | chef's knife | whisk | saucepan | colander | blender | large mixing bowl | brush | large, nonstick griddle | ladle | silicone spatula

FOR THE DIPPING SAUCE

60 ml (2 fl oz) unseasoned rice vinegar

60 ml (2 fl oz) low-sodium soy sauce

2 Tbsp Thai or Vietnamese fish sauce

FOR THE PANCAKES

Sea salt and freshly ground pepper

8 bunches spring onions about 1 kg (2 lb) total weight, root ends trimmed

2 large eggs, lightly beaten

2 tsp low-sodium soy sauce

155 g (5 oz) flour

Peanut, rapeseed, or olive oil for frying

To make the dipping sauce, whisk together the rice vinegar, soy sauce, and fish sauce in a small serving bowl and set aside. *At this point, the dipping sauce can be held for up to 1 day at room temperature.*

To make the pancakes, bring a saucepan of lightly salted water to the boil. Coarsely chop 7 bunches of the spring onions (white and green parts) and finely chop the remaining bunch. (If desired, slice a few onions lengthwise to make a garnish.)

Add the coarsely chopped spring onions to the boiling water and cook until tender, about 5 minutes. Drain briefly, then transfer them to a blender or food processor and process to a smooth purée.

In a large bowl, whisk together the puréed onions, the eggs, 60 ml (2 fl oz) water, and the soy sauce. Gently whisk in the flour until smooth. Add pepper to taste, then stir in the finely chopped spring onions. *At this point, the batter can be held for up to 30 minutes; be sure to stir it well before cooking pancakes and thin it with a little water if it thickens substantially.*

Lightly brush a large, nonstick griddle or a large, well-seasoned cast-iron frying pan with oil and place over medium-high heat. When the cooking surface is hot, ladle 60 ml (2 fl oz) of the batter onto the hot surface, holding the ladle just above the surface to prevent splattering. Using a heatproof silicone spatula, immediately spread the thick batter into a 10-cm (4-in) round. Cook, turning once, until nicely browned on both sides in a lacy pattern, about 3 minutes per side. Repeat to cook the remaining pancakes, brushing the griddle or pan with more oil as needed. You will have about 16 pancakes in all. *At this point, the pancakes can be kept warm in a 95°C (200°F) oven for 15–30 minutes, but they are best served as soon as possible.*

Serve the pancakes on a platter with the bowl of dipping sauce, garnished with lengthwise strips of spring onion, if using.

Springtime dinner

This effortlessly elegant menu blends the comforts of winter, in the form of a hearty lamb braise and a warm citrus dessert, with the fresh spring flavours of asparagus and artichoke.

Roasted Asparagus Salad

Braised Lamb Chops with Artichokes

Spanish-Style Potato Gratin

Meyer Lemon Pudding Cake

White-wine pairing: Albariño or Pinot Grigio
Red-wine pairing: Beaujolais or Côtes du Rhône
Dessert-liqueur pairing: limoncello

SERVES 6

Celebrate the spring theme of this dinner with demure seasonal flowers such as daffodils or tulips, pale-hued table dressings, and delicate, filigreed glassware.

Ahead of time

General party prep

Week of the party

- Assemble the necessary serving pieces:

  Platter for asparagus

  Platter for lamb chops

  Baking dish for gratin

  Gratin dish for pudding cake

  8 cordial glasses

- Select music for party. Keep volume low, to encourage easy conversation. Consider Stravinsky's *The Rite of Spring*, or classic Brazilian bossa nova.
- Plan decorations with flowers and candles.
- Clean the house.
- Determine the seating order and make place cards.

Food and drink

Week of the party

- Visit a wine merchant to select the bottles you need. Pour a light, crisp white, such as a Spanish Albariño or an Italian Pinot Grigio, to balance the complex flavours of the asparagus salad. Spring lamb calls for a light, lively red, such as a Beaujolais or a Grenache blend such as a Côtes du Rhône.

Up to 2 days ahead

- Make a list and go grocery shopping.

Day of the party	After the party starts
Early in the day ■ Agree in advance which host will greet the guests while the other host finishes and serves up the main course, so that there is never a time when both of you are in the kitchen. ■ Arrange flowers and candles around the dining room. ■ Set the table. ■ Set up post-dinner coffee service.	**As guests arrive** ■ One spouse joins the guests in stimulating conversation while the other finishes up the food.
Up to 4 hours ahead ■ Roast asparagus. **Up to 2 hours ahead** ■ Assemble gratin and let stand at room temperature. **Up to 1½ hours ahead** ■ Start lamb chops. ■ Make pudding cake batter and refrigerate. **Up to ½ hour ahead** ■ Bring asparagus to room temperature. ■ Bake gratin. ■ Chill white wine in ice water. **Just before guests arrive** ■ Assemble salad.	**After guests arrive** ■ Offer roasted almonds and crisp pitta bread as appetizers. ■ Make sauce for lamb chops. ■ Rewarm gratin if needed. ■ Put pudding cake in oven and set timer. **At dessert time** ■ If an after-dinner drink is desired, serve small cordial glasses of *limoncello* with the pudding cake.

Roasted Asparagus Salad

preparation **20** minutes | cooking **15** minutes | **6** servings

To snap off the tough, woody ends of asparagus stalks at the correct point, grasp a spear at each end between your thumbs and index fingers. Flex the asparagus gently until you feel the place where it naturally wants to break, then apply more pressure until it snaps away, leaving as much of the tender stem as possible. The additional step of peeling the stalks yields beautiful, bright green spears that cook evenly from top to bottom.

tools | box grater | citrus reamer | chef's knife | salad spinner | vegetable peeler | baking dish | large mixing bowl

1 kg (2 lb) medium-thick asparagus

4 Tbsp (60 ml /2 fl oz) extra-virgin olive oil

Fine sea salt and freshly ground black pepper

Finely grated zest of 1 lemon

1 tsp fresh lemon juice

1 tsp Cognac or brandy

2 Tbsp store-bought tapenade, preferably from the cold case

½ small red onion, sliced paper-thin and separated into pieces

90 g (3 oz) baby rocket leaves, spun dry

Preheat the oven to 230°C (450°F).

To prepare the asparagus, snap off the tough woody ends of the spears and then trim the ends neatly. Using a vegetable peeler, peel the bottom 5 cm (2 in) or so of the spears lengthwise to remove the fibrous exterior. Arrange the asparagus in a baking dish, drizzle with 2 Tbsp of the olive oil, and turn gently to coat evenly. Season with salt and pepper and roast until golden, tender, and slightly wrinkled, about 15 minutes. *At this point, the asparagus can be held for up to 4 hours. Refrigerate it, then remove from the refrigerator about 30 minutes before continuing to let it return to room temperature.*

In a large bowl, combine the lemon zest and juice, Cognac, tapenade, and remaining 2 Tbsp olive oil. Whisk with a fork, then add the red onion and rocket and toss gently to coat and distribute the ingredients.

Transfer the roasted asparagus to a platter and mound the salad mixture over the top. Serve immediately.

Braised Lamb Chops with Artichokes

preparation **10** minutes | cooking **1** hour **40** minutes | **6** servings

This hearty dish is perfect for a chilly spring night, and features two iconic ingredients of the season: spring lamb and artichokes. Lamb shoulder chops are easy to find, easy to cook, and—a boon for the hosts—inexpensive. However, feel free to use smaller, leaner rib chops, in which case you will need to increase the number of chops by about one-third. Sear thinner rib chops for only 2 minutes.

tools | chef's knife | can opener | large sauté pan | tongs | wooden spoon | slotted spoon | large glass measuring pitcher | small saucepan

9–12 lamb shoulder chops, each about 2 cm (¾ in) thick

Fine sea salt and freshly ground pepper

3 Tbsp olive oil

3 cloves garlic, minced

1 Tbsp finely chopped fresh marjoram, plus sprigs for garnish

1 can (445 ml /14½ fl oz) beef stock or consommé

310 ml (10 fl oz) dry white wine or vermouth

3 Tbsp tomato paste

125 g (4 oz) green olives, pitted and halved

2 boxes (315 g/10 oz each) frozen artichoke hearts, thawed

Season the chops generously on both sides with salt and pepper. In a large, heavy sauté pan or a large Dutch oven over medium-high heat, heat the olive oil. When the oil is very hot, add the chops and sear, using tongs to turn once, until golden brown on both sides, about 3 minutes per side. Work in batches to avoid crowding the pan, transferring each batch to a platter.

Stir the garlic and marjoram into the pan with the final batch of chops and cook for 1 minute longer. Return all the chops to the pan (you may have to stack them in 2 layers) and add the stock, wine, and tomato paste. Stir with a wooden spoon to dissolve the paste and scrape up the browned bits from the pan bottom, and bring the liquid to a simmer. Reduce the heat to very low, cover the pan, and simmer very gently for 30 minutes.

After the lamb has been cooking for 30 minutes, turn the chops, rearranging to submerge any chops that started out on top if they are layered in the pan. Scatter the olives over the top, cover the pan, and continue simmering very gently for 30 minutes longer. Add the artichoke hearts and simmer until the lamb is tender, 10–15 minutes longer. *At this point, you can remove the pan from the heat and let it stand on the back of the stove, covered, for up to 30 minutes.*

Using a slotted spoon, transfer the lamb, artichokes, and olives to a platter, cover loosely with foil, and keep warm in a low 95°C (200°F) oven. Pour the braising liquid into a large glass measuring jug or fat separator. Pour or spoon off the fat that rises to the top, then transfer the juices to a small saucepan, place over high heat, and simmer briskly to concentrate the flavours and make a light sauce or jus, about 10 minutes. Pour the jus over the chops and garnish the platter with the marjoram sprigs. Serve at once.

Spanish-Style Potato Gratin

preparation **25** minutes | cooking **55** minutes | standing **15** minutes | **6** servings

This light and pleasing variation on the traditional potato gratin replaces butter and cream with olive oil and stock, and leaves the potato skins on for a rustic look, a touch that nicely complements the Mediterranean style of the menu. The addition of Parmesan adds both savour and a bit of texture.

tools | chef's knife | box grater | large saucepan | colander | mandoline (optional) | large frying pan | small mixing bowl | large oval baking dish | slotted spoon

1.25 kg (2½ lb) white or red potatoes, scrubbed but not peeled

1 Tbsp unsalted butter

1 Tbsp olive oil, plus 60 ml (2 fl oz) for drizzling

2 large onions, very thinly sliced

1 tsp sea salt

½ tsp freshly ground pepper

5 large cloves garlic, minced

1 tsp dried oregano, crumbled

1 tsp dried marjoram, crumbled

Leaves of 8 sprigs fresh thyme, chopped

430 ml (14 fl oz) chicken stock

125 g (4 oz) coarsely grated Parmesan or pecorino cheese (optional)

In a large saucepan, combine the potatoes with enough cold water to cover by 2.5 cm (1 in). Bring to a boil over high heat, then reduce the heat to medium and simmer briskly until the potatoes are tender but still give some resistance when pierced with the tip of a knife, about 10 minutes. Drain thoroughly and let cool. When cool enough to handle, use a very sharp knife or a mandoline to slice the potatoes very thinly, preferably less than 3 mm (⅛ in) thick.

While the potatoes are cooking, in a large, heavy frying pan, melt the butter with the 1 Tbsp olive oil over medium heat. Add the onions and cook, stirring occasionally, until softened, 4–5 minutes. Stir in the salt and pepper and remove the pan from the heat.

Position a rack in the lower third of the oven and preheat to 220°C (425°F). In a small bowl, combine the garlic and herbs and toss together to mix evenly. Drizzle a large (25- to 30-cm /10- to 12-in) oval or rectangular baking dish with a little olive oil and layer one-quarter of the sliced potatoes, slightly overlapping, in the bottom. Scatter one-quarter of the onions evenly over the potatoes, then scatter one-quarter of the garlic-herb mixture over the top and drizzle with a little more olive oil. Repeat to make 3 more layers, finishing with a final drizzle of olive oil. *At this point, the gratin can stand at room temperature for up to 30 minutes.*

Pour the stock around the edges of the dish, taking care not to disturb the herb topping, and cover with foil. Bake until the potatoes are tender when pierced with the tip of a knife, about 30 minutes. Remove the foil. Scatter the cheese over the top, if using. Bake until the top is slightly dried, 5–10 minutes longer. Remove the gratin from the oven and let stand for 10–15 minutes. *At this point, the gratin can stand at room temperature for up to 1 hour.*

If needed, rewarm the gratin for about 15 minutes in a low (95°C /200°F) oven before serving. Serve warm, using a slotted spoon to leave the juices behind.

Meyer Lemon Pudding Cake

preparation **45** minutes | cooking **45** minutes | **6** servings

Pudding cakes are a specialty of the American South but also feature techniques and flavours traditional to French cuisine. This puffed and delicate soufflélike cake is tangy with lemon, yet voluptuously rich at the same time. It is best served directly from the oven, so plan to begin baking it after your guests have arrived, and set a timer so you won't forget about it while you are enjoying dinner.

tools | small saucepan | box grater | chef's knife | citrus reamer | gratin dish | medium saucepan | 2 medium mixing bowls | wooden spoon | large mixing bowl | balloon whisk | electric mixer (optional) | rubber spatula | roasting pan

500 ml (16 fl oz) whole milk

250 g (8 oz) sugar

75 g (2½ oz) flour

⅛ tsp sea salt

3 Tbsp unsalted butter, melted

Finely grated or chopped zest of 2 Meyer lemons (see Note)

125 ml (4 fl oz) fresh Meyer lemon juice (see Note)

4 large eggs, separated

Preheat the oven to 165°C (325°F). Butter a 1.5-litre (48–fl oz) gratin dish or casserole. In a medium saucepan, heat the milk to just below the boil. Watch carefully and do not let it come to a boil; remove from the heat as soon as it begins to simmer. (This is called *scalding* the milk.)

In a medium bowl, stir together the sugar, flour, salt, melted butter, and lemon zest and juice until well mixed. In another medium bowl, whisk the egg yolks until smooth; slowly add the scalded milk, whisking constantly, until the mixture is smooth and well blended.

In a large, spotlessly clean bowl, beat the egg whites with an electric mixer or a balloon whisk until they form stiff, glossy, pointed peaks that hold their shape when the beater is lifted.

Whisk the egg yolk and milk mixture into the lemon mixture until smooth. Gently fold in the egg whites with a rubber spatula. *At this point, the batter can be refrigerated for up to 1½ hours.*

Using a rubber spatula, scoop the batter into the prepared gratin dish and place it inside a slightly larger roasting pan on the oven rack. Carefully pour 2.5 cm (1in) of very hot water into the roasting pan, being careful not to splash. Close the oven door and bake until puffed and evenly golden, about 45 minutes. Set a timer so that you will remember to take it out of the oven toward the very end of the main course. Serve at once, scooping the pudding cake into bowls.

Note: If Meyer lemons are unavailable, substitute the zest of 1 orange and 1 standard lemon for the Meyer lemon zest and 60 ml (2 fl oz) each fresh orange juice and standard lemon juice for the Meyer lemon juice.

Weekend dinner party

This comfort menu, which transforms humble root vegetables into a stylish soup and salad, is finished off with a dessert that tastes like it came straight from a French farmhouse kitchen.

Celery Root Soup

Fennel Salad with Blood Oranges, Rocket, and Shaved Parmesan

Pork Loin with Sweet Mustard Glaze

Spiced Fig and Honey Clafoutis

White-wine pairing: off-dry Riesling
Red-wine pairing: Pinot Noir
Dessert-wine pairing: orange muscat or tawny port

Serve this meal on platters, family style. This not only creates a warm atmosphere at the table, but also means less work for the hosts ferrying plates from the kitchen.

Ahead of time

General party prep

Week of the party

- Assemble the necessary serving pieces:

  Platter for pork loin

  Platter for fennel salad

  Baking dish for clafoutis

- Select music for party. For a stylish choice, nothing beats a classic jazz album. Try John Coltrane's *Blue Train* or Miles Davis's *Kind of Blue.*
- Plan decorations with flowers and candles.
- Clean the house.

Food and drink

Week of the party

- Visit a wine merchant to select the bottles you need. Both the soup and the pork on this menu would be complemented by an off-dry white wine, such as a Washington state or a German Riesling. With the spicy dessert, offer a fruity and full-bodied dessert wine, such as an orange muscat or a tawny port.

Up to 3 days ahead

- Make a list and go grocery shopping.
- If you will be brining the pork—it's worth the small extra effort—make the brine and, before you immerse the pork, be sure the container will fit in your refrigerator.

Day of the party	After the party starts
Early in the day ■ Arrange flowers and candles around the dining room. ■ Set the table. ■ Set up post-dinner coffee service.	**As guests arrive** ■ One spouse takes coats while the other offers the appetizers.
Up to 3 hours ahead ■ Remove the pork from the brine, pat dry, and let come to room temperature. ■ Start soup. ■ Make glaze. ■ Trim fennel and blood oranges. **Up to 2 hours ahead** ■ Soak figs and assemble clafoutis. ■ Slice shallots. ■ Start roasting pork. **Up to ½ hour ahead** ■ Chill white wine in ice water. ■ Assemble salad. ■ Open the windows to encourage a good flow of fresh air, then fry shallots and drain.	**As guests arrive** ■ Offer bowls of wasabi peas and almond-stuffed olives as pre-dinner snacks. **During the party** ■ Once all the guests have arrived, put clafoutis in oven, set timer, and serve dinner. ■ To finish off the menu with an extra vegetable, blanch Swiss chard leaves in boiling water for 2 minutes, then sauté briefly in a little butter.

Celery Root Soup

preparation **30** minutes | cooking **1½** hours | **6–8** first-course servings

Fried shallots make a sensational crisp topping for this autumnal, wine-scented soup, but may easily be omitted for a simpler presentation. You can substitute butternut or other winter squash for the celery root.

tools | chef's knife | vegetable peeler | large saucepan | wooden spatula | blender | whisk (optional) | colander (optional) | heavy wok (optional) | deep-frying thermometer (optional) | skimmer (optional) | tongs (optional) | ladle

3 Tbsp unsalted butter

1 large onion, finely chopped

1 leek, white part only, well washed and finely chopped

1 large sprig fresh thyme, plus leaves for garnish (optional)

500 g (1 lb) celery root (celeriac), peeled and coarsely chopped

500 ml (16 fl oz) dry white wine

750 ml (24 fl oz) vegetable stock

¾ tsp fine sea salt

Freshly ground white pepper

Fried shallot garnish (below; optional)

Melt the butter over medium-low heat in a large saucepan. Add the onion, leek, and thyme sprig and cook gently, stirring often, until the onion and leek are translucent but not browned, about 5 minutes. Add the celery root, partially cover the pan, and cook for 10 minutes. Check occasionally and add a few Tbsp of water if the celery root begins to brown. Add the wine, adjust the heat so that the liquid simmers briskly, and cook until reduced by half, about 20 minutes. Add the stock, partially cover the pan, and let simmer until the celery root is very tender, about 45 minutes. Remove from the heat and let cool, uncovered, for about 5 minutes.

Remove the thyme sprig and, working in batches if necessary, purée the soup in a blender or food processor or with a stick blender until completely smooth. (If using a stand blender, be sure to hold the top on firmly when blending hot liquids.) Return to the pan and stir in the salt and a generous pinch of pepper. Taste and adjust the seasoning. *At this point, the soup can be held for up to 1½ hours.*

Not more than 20 minutes before the soup is ready to serve, make the fried shallots, if using. When ready to serve, reheat the soup gently over medium heat, stirring occasionally, if needed. Ladle into bowls. Garnish with the fried shallots and thyme leaves, if using, and serve hot.

fried shallot garnish Thinly slice 3 large shallots and separate into rings. Whisk together 45 g (1½ oz) flour, ½ tsp paprika, ¼ tsp salt, and a pinch of cayenne. Toss the shallots in the flour mixture, shaking off excess flour. Pour vegetable oil into a heavy wok or saucepan, filling it no more than half full, and heat to 190°C (375°F) on a deep-frying thermometer. Adjust the heat as needed to maintain the temperature. Spread the shallots on a skimmer and lower gently into the hot oil. Fry, nudging occasionally with the skimmer or tongs, until golden but not dark brown, about 1 minute. Transfer to paper towels to drain. Do not hold for more than 20 minutes, or they will get soggy.

Fennel Salad with Blood Oranges, Rocket, and Shaved Parmesan

preparation **20** minutes | **6–8** servings

Fennel salad is crisp and refreshing. A staple in Italy, it is less common elsewhere, and makes a nice change from the standard green salad. To make the salad even more refreshing, slice the vegetables just before serving rather than in advance, and keep the fennel bulbs cold until just before slicing. Note that, unless it is dressed, fennel will discolour if allowed to sit more than 20 minutes after slicing.

tools | chef's knife | salad spinner | large mixing bowl | whisk | vegetable peeler

2 bulbs fennel, stems and fronds removed

4 blood or navel oranges

6 Tbsp (90 ml /3 fl oz) extra-virgin olive oil

2 Tbsp red wine vinegar

¼ tsp fine sea salt

¼ tsp freshly ground pepper

125 g (4 oz) loosely packed rocket leaves, spun dry

60-g (2-oz) chunk Parmesan cheese

Remove any bruised outer leaves from the fennel bulbs and trim off any discoloured bits. Cut a slice off the top and bottom of each orange. Working with 1 orange at a time, stand it on a cut side and carefully slice off the peel and white pith to expose the flesh, following the curve of the fruit with the knife. *At this point, the trimmed fennel and oranges can be held for up to 3 hours.*

Quarter the fennel bulbs, cut out the tough cores, and thinly slice them lengthwise. Slice the oranges crosswise into thin rounds and remove the seeds. *At this point, the sliced fennel and oranges can be held for up to 20 minutes.*

In a large bowl, whisk together the olive oil, vinegar, salt, and pepper. Add the rocket and fennel and toss to coat evenly with the vinaigrette. Mound on a platter and distribute the orange slices over and around the salad. Using a vegetable peeler, shave the Parmesan over the salad in thin curls. Serve the salad as soon as possible; refrigerate if it will be held for more than a few minutes.

Pork Loin with Sweet Mustard Glaze

preparation **10** minutes | standing **30** minutes | cooking **1** hour **25** minutes | resting **10** minutes | **6–8** servings

Look for organically raised pork for superior flavour. If time allows, brine the pork for 1–3 days (see below). Brining yields a noticeably moister and very tasty roast. A generous double roast is made by tying two boneless pork loins together into a uniform cylinder; ask the butcher to do this for you, if possible.

tools | chef's knife | citrus reamer | whisk | small saucepan | roasting pan | roasting rack | brush | instant-read thermometer

One 2-kg (4-lb) boneless centre-cut pork loin roast, about 9 cm (3½ in) in diameter

FOR THE GLAZE

200 g (6½ oz) ginger preserves

75 g (2½ oz) chopped shallot

125 ml (4 fl oz) fresh lemon juice

80 ml (3 fl oz) extra-virgin olive oil

90 g (3 oz) Dijon mustard

Fine sea salt and freshly ground pepper

Fresh sage leaves for garnish (optional)

Pat the pork roast dry with paper towels. Let stand at room temperature for 30 minutes–1 hour before roasting. Preheat the oven to 200°C (400°F).

To make the glaze, whisk together the ginger preserves, shallot, lemon juice, olive oil, and mustard in a small saucepan. Pour half of the glaze into a small saucepan.

Line a roasting pan with foil. Place the roast, fat side up, on a rack in the roasting pan. Brush generously on all sides with the glaze from the bowl and season with salt and pepper. Roast the pork for 25 minutes, then reduce the oven temperature to 165°C (325°F) and roast for about 1 hour longer, basting occasionally with the glaze from the bowl. When an instant-read thermometer inserted into the thickest part registers 63°C (145°F), the roast is done. (The timing will depend not on the weight, but on the thickness of the roast; a roast with a smaller diameter will take substantially less time.) Remove from the oven and let the pork rest on the rack, loosely covered with foil, for 10 minutes. This resting will allow the pork juices to redistribute evenly throughout the roast, resulting in moister slices.

While the pork is resting, place the glaze in the saucepan over medium heat and bring to a simmer to warm, then remove from the heat. Transfer the roast to a cutting board. Using a sharp knife, cut the pork into slices 12 mm (½ in) thick. Serve the pork with a generous drizzle of the glaze, garnished with sage if desired.

brining the pork Bring 750 ml (24 fl oz) water to a simmer and stir in 125 g (4 oz) sea salt and 105 g (3½ oz) brown sugar until dissolved. In a tall, nonaluminum container, combine the salt mixture with 1 small onion, sliced; 2 bay leaves; 10 peppercorns; and 1.25 litres (40 fl oz) very cold water. Submerge the roast in the brine completely and refrigerate for at least 1 day and preferably 3 days. Remove the pork from the brine 30 minutes–1 hour before roasting time.

Spiced Fig and Honey Clafoutis

standing **45** minutes | preparation **20** minutes | cooking **35** minutes | **6–8** servings

Clafoutis (pronounced klah-foo-tee) is a rustic, farmhouse-style French dessert that is traditionally made with fresh cherries, usually with the stones still inside to prevent the running juices from turning the batter pink. Its easy preparation and attractive presentation have made it popular outside France in recent years.

tools | chef's knife | box grater | small saucepan | small mixing bowl | oval baking dish | large mixing bowl | whisk | slotted spoon | fine-mesh sieve

80 ml (3 fl oz) honey

250 ml (8 fl oz) very hot water

500 g (1 lb) dried figs, halved lengthwise

2 large eggs plus 1 large egg yolk

90 g/3 oz granulated sugar

45 g (1½ oz) flour

¼ tsp freshly grated nutmeg

¼ tsp ground allspice

¼ tsp ground cinnamon

310 ml (10 fl oz) double cream

4 Tbsp (60 g/2 oz) unsalted butter, melted

45 g (1½ oz) coarsely chopped walnuts (optional)

Icing sugar for dusting

In a small bowl, dissolve the honey in the hot water and add the figs. Toss and let stand for 45 minutes to plump the fruit, tossing occasionally.

Preheat the oven to 200°C (400°F). Butter the bottom and sides of a 30-cm (12-in) oval or similar-sized baking dish. Sprinkle with granulated sugar and tap to shake out the excess.

In a large mixing bowl, whisk together the eggs and egg yolk, then whisk in the granulated sugar. Add the flour, nutmeg, allspice, and cinnamon and stir to combine, then stir in the cream and melted butter until well blended.

Using a slotted spoon, transfer the figs to the baking dish, spreading them evenly. Whisk the honey liquid remaining in the bowl into the egg batter. Scatter the walnuts over the figs, if using, and pour the batter evenly over the top. Bake until puffy and golden, about 35 minutes. Serve warm, dusting each serving with a little powdered sugar.

dusting with sugar To give a dessert a pretty sprinkling of powdered sugar, put the sugar in a sieve and tap the sieve gently as you move it over each serving.

OUTDOOR ENTERTAINING

Almost no dining experience is more memorable and enjoyable than an outdoor meal at which the food is delicious, the weather is cooperative, the conversation is sparkling, and the guests are relaxed.

Because they are invariably casual, festive, and fun for everyone, alfresco celebrations appeal to adults and kids alike (and to hosts, too). Whether you are staging your party in your back garden, on your deck or patio, or at a local park or beach, you will need to do a little more planning than you would for a similar event held indoors. But careful forethought and some creativity on your part will help ensure that nothing—neither burning sun, nor sudden downpour, nor the nuisance of mosquitoes, nor smoking barbeque—will ruin your delightful outdoor party.

OUTDOOR TABLE SETTINGS

If you don't have an outdoor dining table and/or an adequate number of chairs, buffet-style serving will probably work best for your party. This way, guests can serve themselves and perch, plate on lap, on whatever seating you can make available: deck chairs, a garden bench, or indoor chairs surrounding card tables outfitted with tablecloths. The buffet table can be decorated or can hold an attractive centrepiece that matches the party's theme, drawing guests' interest toward the table and the food. Wrap cutlery in napkins and place in small buckets, vases, or other containers at the far end of the buffet, so guests don't have to juggle both their plate and their cutlery as they serve themselves.

OUTDOOR LIGHTING

Your guests are your first consideration when lighting for evening outdoor parties. You need to make sure that walkways and porch steps will be safely navigated, and that everyone can easily see the foods that they'll be eating. But lighting involves more than practicality. An outdoor setting often limits other decorating possibilities, so that the lighting you choose takes on a more significant role than simply illuminating the space.

If gentle candlelight is the effect you're after, you'll need hurricane lamps, clear vases, or other shields to protect the flame from wind and your garden from flame. Consider tiki torches and oil lamps to create a festive glow. Electric lights are another charming possibility: strings of lights are available in many styles, from a simple strand of white bulbs to strings of ornate lanterns. Make sure any extension cords you use are approved for outdoor use and are securely taped down.

Fresh-air festivities

First, take a critical look at your available space. If you have a deck, is it large enough for both the pre-dinner appetizers and the sit-down main course, or would it be better to serve aperitifs on an adjoining lawn or patio space? Think about extras that will provide added atmosphere and comfort, such as lanterns, heaters, citronella candles, and umbrellas that can provide shade on a hot afternoon or protection from a passing rain cloud.

Beyond your own garden, there are also many public places, such as parks and beaches, that are appropriate for simple or elaborate picnic-style celebrations. Be sure to check regulations, hours, and whether or not glass bottles and alcohol are allowed before you settle on a venue. If you will be transporting food over a long distance or for any length of time, keep food safety in mind. Hot foods may not be practical, but if you do decide to serve a hot main dish, for example, you may need to rent or buy equipment, such as a thermos or a chafing dish, to keep it hot en route or to reheat it once you're at your destination. If a dish containing meat or poultry will be served at room temperature, keep it chilled until just before leaving the house and carry it in a cooler, so that it doesn't spend more than a couple of hours at ambient temperature before serving. Keep cold dishes, such as ceviche, soups, and many salads, in sealed containers over ice.

Wild weather

Begin checking the forecast five days ahead of the party, and if there is any hint of rain, make contingency plans for what to do if the heavens open on your event. This might include clearing space for the table under a covered porch, or, if the party is formal and important, hiring a tent from an equipment-rental company. Consider how to keep the tablecloth secured to the table in case of strong winds: creatively used, clips or weights can be part of your decorations.

With a plan in mind for dealing with both rain and strong winds, the two of you will not be plunged into a state of confusion if the weather turns against you. Instead, you'll find a way to make it fun: light tiki torches, turn up the music, and dance under a porch or tent. The party goes on!

Grill parties

There is some sort of primeval imperative that can overtake even the most civilized spouse when the subject of grilling comes up. The image of the grill master standing over a fire—wreathed by smoke, imposing set of tongs in hand—while cooking dinner for friends becomes a powerful lure. If your spouse is subject to these hallucinations, do not stand in his or her way. Confine yourself to the role of dutiful cohost and busy yourself passing drinks and bringing out side dishes while your mate holds court at the grill.

Getting ready to grill

Once you've decided that the season and the occasion are right for grilling, choose a menu in which only one of the items must be grilled at a time, and ideally one in which much of the preparation for the other courses is out of the way before grilling begins. Here is where setting the table and assembling all the other party elements ahead of time will really pay off.

Both gas and charcoal grills have their passionate fans. There is no doubt that food grilled over charcoal or even hardwood has a smokier flavour, but there's also no beating the convenience and cleanliness of gas. Depending on your level of devotion to outdoor cooking, you may decide to acquire both.

Gauge the direction of the wind on the morning of the get-together. If your grill is portable, wheel it to the downwind side of the party area, so that guests in their summer finery are not surrounded by billows of smoke, coughing politely as they sip their aperitifs. If your grill is built in, place the dining table and hors d'oeuvre buffet as far from it as possible and, preferably, upwind.

To prevent midcooking crises, get your grill ready in advance. First, if it's been months since you've used it, discard any old ashes, check the gas level, and give the grill rack a scrub with a wire brush to banish any remnants of parties past. After cleaning the rack, rub it top and bottom with paper towels soaked in vegetable oil, rubbing the oil in well and then blotting any excess. This will prevent the food from sticking, which can put a real damper on the grill master's enthusiasm midparty (and that of the dutiful cohost, too).

GRILLING BASICS

Even if one or both of you think grilling is a breeze, you should bone up on the mechanics before you cook for a hungry crowd: how to grill over direct and indirect heat, how to check the temperature of the fire before you put the food on, and how to control flare-ups.

One essential strategy is to build the fire or light the burners to allow for grilling at different temperatures. Make the grill hot on one side, medium on the other, and reserve an area without coals or heat. This way, food can be moved to a cooler part of the grill if flames are shooting up or if food is in danger of cooking too quickly. A spray bottle of water may also help you control flare-ups. And because the heat level of a grill is wildly variable, be aware that grilling recipe times must be considered guidelines: if you are not adept at judging doneness by touch, use a thermometer or cut into the meat if you have any doubts about the degree of doneness.

TOOLS FOR OUTDOOR COOKING

- WIRE BRUSH
- LONG-HANDLED TONGS
- LONG-HANDLED BRUSH
- PROTECTIVE MITTS
- CHIMNEY OR STARTER FLUID
- MATCHES
- CHARCOAL OR PROPANE
- WOOD CHIPS FOR FLAVOUR
- SKEWERS
- SPRAY BOTTLE
- PAPER TOWELS
- GRILL OR OVEN THERMOMETER
- INSTANT-READ THERMOMETER

Margaritaville

The theme of this summertime menu is definitely tropical, with simple and satisfying food and drink offering bright colours, assertive flavours, and plenty of sizzle.

Classic Margarita

Cuban Mojito

The Best Guacamole

Scallop and Mango Ceviche

Key Lime Cheesecake

SERVES 8–10

This is the perfect party for the first hot and sunny Saturday of the summer, when your friends have been covered up with wool and flannel for months and are ready to haul out the flip-flops and sarongs.

Ahead of time

General party prep

Week of the party

- Assemble the necessary serving pieces:
  - *8–10 each old-fashioned and highball glasses*
  - *Ice buckets and jugs for citrus juices at bar*
  - *16–20 cocktail plates for ceviche and cheesecake*
  - *Serving bowl for guacamole*
  - *2 serving bowls or baskets for chips*
- Select music for party: mariachi or Cuban jazz.
- Plan outdoor lighting and bar setup, including supplies for printing out and posting drink recipes.
- Spruce up outdoor area where the party will take place, and make sure you have enough tables and chairs (or other seating).

Food and drink

Week of the party

- Visit a good off licence to stock up on tequila, orange rum, triple sec, and other bar needs.

3 days ahead

- Check your market for ripe avocados. If they are all unripe, buy some now and let ripen in a paper bag. If only ripe avocados are available now, wait until closer to the party to buy them. Check for elusive Key limes, too.

Up to 1 day ahead

- Make a list and go grocery shopping.

Up to 12 hours ahead

- Squeeze the citrus juices for cocktails, ceviche, and cheesecake; make and refrigerate cheesecake.
- Make ceviche; toss mixture every 2–3 hours.

Day of the party

Early in the day

- Set up a bar in your outdoor space. At the bar, set up glass or clear plastic ice buckets to display festive tequila and rum bottles, and glass jugs for freshly squeezed citrus juices.
- Arrange seating and small tables to encourage conversation groups.
- If planning a self-serve bar, print out cocktail recipes on colourful cards; post above the bar area, place inside clear plastic table tents, or mount on place-card clips.
- Set up a food buffet for bowls of guacamole and chips at the opposite end of the outdoor space from the bar area (to encourage movement).

Up to 6 hours ahead

- Squeeze citrus juices and make ceviche and cheesecake if not done the day before.

Up to 4 hours ahead

- Assemble bar and cocktail garnishes; refrigerate mint leaves and lime wedges.

Up to 2 hours ahead

- Start guacamole (do not add avocados yet).

Up to ½ hour ahead

- If there is room, chill glasses in the freezer.
- Complement the party menu with roasted pistachio nuts, jicama sticks sprinkled with chilli powder, and cubes of jalapeño Jack cheese on colourful toothpicks. Arrange on small platters and place around party area.

After the party starts

During the party

- Continually clear away used napkins and glasses to keep the party area attractive.

As guests arrive

- Mash avocados into guacamole.
- Stir mango into ceviche and put in lettuce cups.
- Start mixing cocktails, or usher guests to the bar to show them they can mix their own.

During the party

- One host can pass platters of ceviche in lettuce cups, to encourage the flow of people around the garden. Or, ask a usually shy guest to pass the platter.

Classic Margarita

preparation **5** minutes | mixing **1** minute | **1** serving

There are whole books devoted to the preparation of the margarita, one of the most popular cocktails in North America. Here is a classic recipe for the legendary drink.

tools | paring knife | citrus reamer | old-fashioned glass | small plate | cocktail shaker | jigger

1 lime wedge

Sea salt

Ice cubes

1 jigger (45 ml /1½ fl oz) silver tequila

1 pony (30 ml /1 fl oz) triple sec

2 Tbsp fresh lime juice

Rub the lime wedge around the rim of an old-fashioned glass. Pour salt into a small plate to a depth of 6 mm (¼ in). Dip the moistened rim of the glass in the salt to coat. Set the prepared glass and the lime wedge aside.

Fill a cocktail shaker half full with ice. Add the tequila, triple sec, and lime juice. Cover with the lid and shake vigorously for 10–20 seconds. Fill the prepared glass with fresh ice and strain in the cocktail. Squeeze the remaining juice from the lime wedge into the glass, drop in the wedge, and serve immediately.

blended margarita Purists frown on this blended version, yet it has many fans. Prepare the glass as described above; combine tequila, triple sec, and lime juice in a blender with two cubes of ice and blend at high speed until smooth.

Cuban Mojito

preparation **5** minutes | mixing **2** minutes | **1** serving

The mojito. *Not since the margarita was introduced in the 1930s has a cocktail so captured the hearts and minds of a generation.*

tools | citrus reamer | highball glass | cocktail stirrer | muddler | jigger | blender

Juice of ½ lime (about 1½ Tbsp)

1 tsp caster sugar

1 Tbsp fresh mint leaves, plus 1 sprig

Crushed ice

2 ponies (60 ml/2 fl oz) orange rum

Sparkling water for topping

Combine the lime juice and sugar in a highball glass and stir until the sugar has dissolved. Add the mint leaves and muddle the ingredients by mashing them firmly against the base of the glass with a muddler, pestle, or the back of a small wooden spoon. Fill the glass with crushed ice and pour in the rum. Stir again and top with a splash of sparkling water. Garnish with the mint sprig and serve immediately.

crushed ice If you run short of purchased crushed ice and you need to make some in a hurry, here's how: wrap whole cubes in a clean towel and bash them with a mallet or the back of a large ladle.

The Best Guacamole

preparation **20** minutes | **8–10** cocktail-party servings

Guacamole has been a favourite of so many for so long that it has often been "improved," sometimes to the point that it no longer resembles the original Mexican dish. This honest version does not try to gild the lily: Guacamole should be about nothing more than great avocado flavour, crunch and tang from white onions, and heat to taste from the chilies. Coriander adds a crucial fresh note.

tools | chef's knife | large mixing bowl | vegetable peeler (optional) | mandoline (optional) | deep-frying thermometer (optional) | wok (optional) | skimmer (optional)

75 g (2½ oz) chopped white onion

30 g (1 oz) loosely packed fresh coriander leaves, finely chopped

2–3 serrano chillis, seeded and chopped

1 tsp sea salt

6 ripe avocados, about 1.5 kg (3 lb) total weight

½ lime

37 g (1¼ oz) finely chopped shallots

15 g (½ oz) loosely packed fresh coriander leaves

Root vegetable chips (left) or tortilla chips for serving

In a large glass or ceramic bowl, combine the onion, coriander, chillis to taste, and salt. *At this point, the onion mixture can be covered and refrigerated for up to 2 hours.*

At serving time, cut the avocados in half and remove the stones. Scoop out the flesh and mash it into the onion mixture with a fork, turning it over from the bottom so that the seasonings are well distributed. The avocado should not be mashed to smoothness; the guacamole should still have a coarse texture. Transfer to a serving bowl and squeeze the juice from the lime half over the top. Scatter the shallots and coriander leaves over the top and serve at once, along with plenty of tortilla chips.

root vegetable chips Peel 2 yams (orange-fleshed sweet potatoes), 2 parsnips, 5 carrots, and 3 beets. Using a mandoline or a sharp chef's knife, slice them crosswise as thinly as possible. Clip a deep-frying thermometer to the side of a heavy wok or large saucepan, or set up an electric deep-fryer. Line baking sheets with double layers of paper towels. Pour vegetable oil into the pan to fill it no more than half full and heat the oil to 190°C (375°F). (For a wok or saucepan, use your most powerful burner and, if possible, place at the back of the stove for safety.) Adjust the heat as needed to maintain the temperature at 190°C (375°F).

Working in batches to avoid crowding, spread the vegetable slices on a skimmer or in the fryer basket and lower gently into the hot oil. Fry, nudging occasionally with the skimmer or tongs, until golden, 4–5 minutes. Using the skimmer, transfer to the paper towels, sprinkle with sea salt, and let drain until serving.

Scallop and Mango Ceviche

preparation **20** minutes | marinating **6** hours | **8–10** cocktail-party servings

Try to find sea scallops for this dish. If smaller bay scallops are the only option, arrange them on a plate lined with a paper towel, then top with another towel and plate and press for 20 minutes to extract as much water as possible. If frozen, thaw this way for 1–2 hours in the refrigerator before mixing with the citrus juices.

tools | chef's knife | citrus reamer | mixing bowl | wooden spoon | slotted spoon

625 g (1¼ lb) bay scallops or sea scallops (see Note)

250 ml (8 fl oz) fresh lime juice (6–7 limes)

90 ml (3 fl oz) fresh orange juice

1½ Tbsp finely chopped fresh coriander

2 tsp sea salt

¾ tsp red chilli flakes

4 drops of Tabasco sauce, or to taste

2 or 3 heads butter or Cobb lettuce, chilled

1 ripe mango, peeled, stoned, and cut into smallish pieces

Best-quality lemon-scented or plain extra-virgin olive oil for drizzling

Julienned red pepper (capsicum) for garnish (optional)

With your fingers, pull off the hard side muscle (called the adductor) from the side of each scallop, if needed. Dice the scallops. In a glass or ceramic bowl, combine the scallops, lime juice, orange juice, coriander, salt, chilli flakes, and Tabasco. Toss gently and cover with cling film. Refrigerate for at least 6 and up to 12 hours to allow the scallops to "cook" gently in the acidic juices, tossing the ingredients every 2–3 hours.

When ready to serve, remove the outer leaves from the lettuce heads until you reach the pale inner hearts. Reserve the outer leaves for another use and separate the hearts into leaves, selecting 16–20 of the smaller, best-shaped leaves to use as cups for the ceviche. Gently stir the mango into the scallops. Using a slotted spoon, mound the ceviche in the lettuce cups. Drizzle with the olive oil, garnish with the red pepper, and serve immediately.

Note: Raw or cooked peeled prawns, or any finned whitefish—such as very fresh striped sea bass or halibut—can be substituted for the scallops.

Key Lime Cheesecake

preparation **40** minutes | cooking **35** minutes | chilling **2** hours | **8–10** servings

Tiny Key limes are sometimes available in markets, but standard Persian limes, the most widely available variety, are a fine substitute (and are quicker to squeeze). Whichever type you use, your work with the citrus reamer will pay off: these tart little cheesecake squares make a welcome finish to this lime-centric menu.

tools | small saucepan | box grater | citrus juicer | rectangular baking dish | food processor | mixing bowl | wire rack | chef's knife

FOR THE CRUST

Vegetable oil spray

24 crackers

90 g (3 oz) sugar

6 Tbsp (90 g /3 oz) unsalted butter, melted

FOR THE FILLING

500 g (1 lb) cream cheese, softened, or whipped cream cheese

125 g (4 oz) sugar

2 large eggs

1 Tbsp finely grated lime zest

125 ml (4 fl oz) fresh Key lime juice

Very thin lime slices for garnish

Preheat the oven to 165°C (325°F). Lightly spray the bottom and sides of an 28-by-18-cm (11-by-7-in) or similar-sized baking dish with oil.

To make the crust, in a food processor, combine the crackers and sugar and process until the mixture resembles a fine meal. Transfer to a bowl and add the melted butter. Stir with a fork to blend thoroughly. Press the mixture evenly into the bottom (but not up the sides) of the prepared baking dish.

Wash and dry the food processor. To make the filling, combine the cream cheese, sugar, eggs, and lime zest and juice in the food processor and pulse until smooth. Pour the filling over the crust and jiggle the pan a little to help level the filling. Bake until slightly puffed and set, about 35 minutes. Let cool completely in the pan on a wire rack, then cover with cling film and refrigerate until well chilled, at least 2 hours and up to 12 hours.

Using a sharp knife, cut the cheesecake into 16–20 rectangles. To get a clean cut, dip the knife into hot water and wipe it clean and dry before each cut. Garnish each serving with lime slices.

Mediterranean mezze

Choose to serve this harmonious medley of intriguing small plates as a buffet for a stand-up party or as an exotic sit-down dinner, with equally enjoyable results.

Labne

Marinated Beef Kebabs

Grilled Aubergine with Feta

Chickpea Salad with Mint

Citrus-Scented Grapes and Melon

White-wine pairing: retsina or Vouvray
Red-wine pairing: Shiraz or Syrah

For this meal, provide richly coloured dishes and napkins, gilded Moroccan tea glasses, jewel-toned enameled forks, and woven baskets for the disposal of skewers.

Ahead of time

General party prep

Week of the party

- Assemble the necessary serving pieces:

  Platters for labne, *beef kebabs, and aubergine rolls*

  Platter or bowl for chickpea (garbanzo bean) salad

  Serving bowl for fruit salad

  6–8 place settings or cocktail plates and napkins

  6–8 dessert place settings and demitasse cups
- Select music for party.
- Plan outdoor lighting such as hanging candles, and decorations with fruit and flowers.
- Spruce up outdoor area where the party will take place, making sure you have enough outdoor tables and chairs (or other seating, such as floor pillows).

Food and drink

Week of the party

- Visit a wine merchant to select the bottles you need. With the *labne,* offer a Greek white, perhaps a retsina—with its unique, strange aroma of pine resin—if you think your guests will be intrigued by its unusual character. (If you choose retsina, provide an alternative white, such as a lush Vouvray, just in case.) The meaty and flavourful main course and smoky aubergine side dish call for a powerful, spicy, rich-hued red, such as an Australian Shiraz or a California Syrah.

Up to 3 days ahead

- Make a list and go grocery shopping.

  Drain yoghurt for *labne,* if needed.

Up to 2 days ahead

- Make *labne;* turn over to coat with oil occasionally.
- Cook chickpeas for chickpea salad.

Day of the party

Early in the day

- If serving buffet style, set up a buffet table in your outdoor space.
- If serving as a sit-down dinner, set the table. Alternatively, arrange seating around small tables to encourage conversation groups.
- Decorate buffet table or side table with pyramids of oranges and vases of large, brightly coloured tissue-paper flowers.

Up to 6 hours ahead

- Marinate beef.
- Make fruit salad.
- Cook chickpeas if not done ahead.

Up to 1 hour ahead

- Soak skewers, if needed, then thread beef on skewers.

Up to ½ hour ahead

- Prepare grill.
- Chill wine in ice water.
- Assemble *labne* platter.
- Finish chickpea salad.
- Grill aubergine (this can be done earlier in the day).

Just before the party starts

- Assemble aubergine rolls.

After the party starts

During the party

- If guests are seated for the meal, offer finger bowls of warm rosewater at the table.

As guests arrive

- One host welcomes guests and passes *labne,* while the other host grills beef kebabs.

During the party

- Bring chilled wine to the table and start the buffet or, if it's a sit-down affair, seat guests and pour ice water.

At the end of the evening

- Offer strong, sweet black coffee in demitasse cups. Using a French press would help approximate thick Turkish coffee.

Labne

preparation **25** minutes | draining **12** hours | **6–8** appetizer servings

Labne, *a luscious, thick cheese made from yoghurt, is enjoyed throughout the eastern Mediterranean and Middle East. If your* labne *does not seem firm enough to form into balls (which may happen if strained Greek yoghurt is unavailable, or if your yoghurt contains an emulsifier), spread the drained yoghurt on a large plate about 2.5cm (1in) thick, using circular motions with a large spoon. Use the back of the spoon to create plenty of peaks and troughs, to capture the olive oil. Drizzle with the olive oil, season with salt and pepper, sprinkle with the sumac, and then serve.*

tools | chef's knife | garlic press (optional) | fine-mesh sieve | cheesecloth (muslin) | 2 mixing bowls | 2 spoons

1 carton (545 g /17½ oz) Greek strained plain yoghurt or (560 g /18 oz) plain full-fat yoghurt without added gelatin

2 large cloves garlic, finely chopped or crushed through a press

2 tsp finely chopped fresh parsley

¼ tsp red chilli flakes, or to taste

¼ tsp ground cumin

60 ml (2 fl oz) best-quality extra-virgin olive oil

¼ tsp sumac or red za'atar (see Note)

Salt and freshly ground pepper

Pitta wedges or crusty bread for serving

If you are unable to find Greek yoghurt, you will need to strain your regular yoghurt to thicken it. Line a fine-mesh sieve with a double layer of damp cheesecloth (muslin) and place over a bowl. Pour the yoghurt into the sieve and refrigerate. Let drain for 12 hours or up to 3 days to make yoghurt cheese.

In a dry bowl, use a fork to whisk together the garlic, parsley, chilli flakes, and cumin. Whisk this mixture into the yoghurt cheese. Pour the olive oil over a platter and scatter the sumac evenly over the oil. Using 2 spoons, scoop out about 1 Tbsp of the strained yoghurt and form it into a rough ball. Transfer to the platter. Turn very gently to coat on all sides with the flavoured oil. Repeat to make more balls until all the mixture has been used. *At this point, the* labne *may be covered and refrigerated for up to 2 days; gently turn over the balls occasionally, and drizzle them with a little more olive oil if desired.*

To serve, season with salt and pepper and surround with the pitta wedges.

Note: Sumac, a deep red, powdery spice with a sour taste, is used in Middle Eastern cooking. Red za'atar, a spice blend that contains sumac, is popular in the same region. If neither is available, double the quantity of cumin.

Marinated Beef Kebabs

preparation **30** minutes | marinating **1½** hours | cooking **15** minutes per batch | **6–8** servings

All across the Middle East there is a rich tradition of kebab style grilled meats. Here, the juice of the onion acts as a marinade, tenderising and adding flavour to the beef along with the tart tang of vinegar. The fresh herbs add a bright colour and flavour that makes this an attractive centrepiece platter. The ease of eating meat as a kebab, rather than with a knife and fork, also makes it ideal for a stand-up party.

tools | chef's knife | food processor | baking dish | 40 small bamboo skewers | grill (optional) | wire grill brush (optional) | tongs

1.75 kg (3½ lb) boneless sirloin steak, trimmed of excess fat

1 large onion, halved

125 ml (4 fl oz) red wine vinegar

3 cloves garlic, sliced

30 g (1 oz) firmly packed fresh basil leaves, plus 5 large or 8–10 smaller leaves, cut into chiffonade (below)

1 tsp sea salt

½ tsp freshly ground pepper

Vegetable oil for brushing (optional)

2 Tbsp chopped fresh coriander (optional)

Cut the sirloin into 2.5-cm (1-in) cubes. Coarsely chop one onion half and place it in a food processor with the vinegar, garlic, basil, salt, and pepper. Pulse to a smooth purée. Transfer the purée to a glass or ceramic baking dish, add the beef cubes, and toss to coat evenly. Cover with cling film and let stand at room temperature for 1½ hours, or refrigerate for at least 3 hours and up to 6 hours. Return to room temperature before cooking. Meanwhile, soak skewers in water to cover for at least 30 minutes.

Prepare a fire in a charcoal grill, preheat a gas grill to medium-high, or preheat the grill. If using a charcoal or gas grill, scrape the rack clean with a wire brush, if necessary, and use paper towels to brush it lightly with oil. Position the grill rack or grill pan about 10 cm (4 in) from the heat source.

Separate the layers of the remaining onion half and cut as many 2.5-cm (1-in) squares from each single-layer piece as possible. Drain the skewers. Starting and ending with the sirloin, thread 2 cubes of beef onto each skewer, alternating with 1 piece of onion. Press the ingredients firmly together to help them stay moist during cooking. You may not need to use all of the skewers.

When the grill is hot, arrange the assembled kebabs on the grill rack directly over the heat or on the grill pan and grill, turning with tongs, for about 3 minutes on each of all 4 sides for medium-rare, or 12–15 minutes total, depending on the heat of the fire. (The meat should be browned but not tough to the touch. Move the kebabs to a cooler area after the first minute if the coals flare up or the kebabs are in danger of charring.)

Transfer kebabs to a platter, scatter with the basil chiffonade and with the coriander, if using, and serve.

making chiffonade Stack basil or other leaves, roll tightly lengthwise (like a cigar), and finely slice them crosswise to make a chiffonade.

Grilled Aubergine with Feta

preparation **25** minutes | cooking **10** minutes | **6–8** side-dish servings

Be sure not to grill the aubergine slices for so long that they fall apart, or they won't hold the feta mixture. This dish makes an easy finger-food appetizer if your guests will be standing during the event.

tools | chef's knife | grill | wire grill brush (optional) | 2 baking sheets | brush | tongs | mixing bowl | cocktail sticks (optional)

Extra-virgin olive oil for brushing

Sea salt and freshly ground pepper

4 slender aubergines, about 185 g (6 oz) each

155 g (5 oz) crumbled feta cheese

125 g (4 oz) whole-milk ricotta cheese

2 tsp finely chopped fresh basil, or as needed

⅛ tsp ground allspice, or as needed

Prepare a fire in a charcoal grill or preheat a gas grill to medium-low. Scrape the rack clean with a wire brush, if necessary, and use paper towels to brush it lightly with olive oil. Position the grill rack about 10 cm (4 in) from the fire. Brush 2 baking sheets with olive oil and sprinkle with salt and pepper.

Trim the ends of the aubergine and slice them lengthwise just under 6 mm (¼ in) thick. Place on the prepared baking sheets; brush the aubergine slices with olive oil and season with salt and pepper.

When the grill is hot, arrange the aubergine slices on the rack and grill, turning once with tongs, until slightly softened and golden but not falling apart, about 10 minutes total. Return to the baking sheets in a single layer. *At this point, you can let the grilled aubergine stand at room temperature for up to 2 hours, or cover with cling film and refrigerate for up to 6 hours. If the aubergine is refrigerated, it will be easier to assemble the aubergine rolls while the aubergine is still cold, but bring the rolls to room temperature before serving.*

In a bowl, stir together with a fork the feta, ricotta, basil, allspice, ½ tsp salt, and a generous grinding of pepper. Place a scant 1 Tbsp of the filling at the wider end of each aubergine slice and roll into a snug cylinder. Secure with a cocktail stick if necessary. Stand the rolls, open side up, on a platter. Sprinkle with a little more allspice and chopped basil, if desired, and serve.

Chickpea Salad with Mint

preparation **30** minutes | cooking **1½** hours | standing **1** hour **20** minutes | **6–8** servings

Earthy and satisfying, chickpeas are enjoyed on all sides of the Mediterranean, appearing in salads, stews, and soups from Cannes to Crete. You might also try small white (navy), pinto, or black beans or lentils. To save time, you can use rinsed and drained canned chickpeas here—but the ones you cook yourself will have a superior texture and flavour.

tools | chef's knife | saucepan | colander | 2 mixing bowls

375 g (12 oz) dried chickpeas (garbanzo beans)

½ small onion

1 sprig fresh thyme

Salt and freshly ground pepper

80 ml (3 fl oz) extra-virgin olive oil

80 ml (3 fl ozl) red wine vinegar, plus extra to taste

3 or 4 cloves garlic, minced

1 tsp ground cumin

1 small red onion, diced

7 g (¼ oz) chopped fresh mint, plus mint chiffonade (page 101) for garnish (optional)

Pick over the chickpeas, discard any misshapen ones, and then rinse and drain well. In a saucepan, combine the chickpeas with water to cover by 5 cm (2 in). Bring to the boil over high heat and let boil for 2 minutes. Remove from the heat, cover, and let stand for 1 hour.

Drain the chickpeas well and return them to the pan. Add water to cover by 7.5 cm (3 in), the onion half, and the thyme sprig and bring to a simmer over medium heat. Cook, uncovered, until the chickpeas are tender but not falling apart, about 1¼ hours, adding 1½ teaspoons salt during the last 10 minutes of cooking.

Drain the chickpeas and discard the onion half and thyme sprig. Transfer the chickpeas to a bowl of cold water. Slip the skins from the chickpeas by rubbing them between your fingers, then drain well. *At this point, the chickpeas can be covered and refrigerated for up to 2 days.*

In a small bowl, whisk together the olive oil, vinegar, garlic, cumin, and salt and pepper to taste. Add to the chickpeas and toss together to coat evenly. Add the red onion and toss gently. Let stand for 20 minutes at room temperature.

Taste the salad and adjust the seasoning with more salt, pepper, and vinegar, if necessary. Add the chopped mint and toss to mix well. Transfer the salad to a platter or individual plates. Garnish with mint chiffonade, if desired, and serve.

Citrus-Scented Grapes and Melon

preparation **30** minutes | cooking **10** minutes | chilling **2** hours | **6–8** dessert servings

Orange flower water—one of the traditional flavourings for Turkish delight—is a Middle Eastern pantry staple. It is available in the baking section of well-stocked supermarkets and in gourmet and Middle Eastern markets. It carries a strong, perfumelike scent and flavour, and a little goes a long way. To remove the brown skins from shelled pistachio nuts, rub them in a kitchen towel.

tools | citrus reamer | chef's knife | small saucepan | mixing bowl | vegetable peeler | sieve | medium saucepan | heatproof bowl

1 lemon

185 g (6 oz) sugar

3 Tbsp fresh lemon juice

½ tsp orange flower water

1 small, ripe cantaloupe, about 1.5 kg (3 lb), halved and seeded

315 g (10 oz) seedless green grapes, halved

60 g (2 oz) unsalted pistachio nuts, coarsely chopped

Orange zest strips for garnish (optional)

Bring a small saucepan of water to the boil. Have ready a bowl of ice water. Cut the zest from the lemon in wide strips and then cut into matchstick-sized strips. When the water comes to a boil, add the zest and blanch for 1 minute. Scoop up the zest with a sieve and place it in the ice water to stop the cooking. Drain the zest.

Combine 250 ml (8 fl oz) plus 2 Tbsp water, the sugar, and the lemon juice in a medium saucepan. Place over low heat, cover, and heat, swirling the pan occasionally, until the sugar dissolves. Uncover the pan, raise the heat to medium-high, and bring to the boil. Add the blanched lemon zest and adjust the heat to achieve a gentle simmer. Cook until the syrup is very slightly thickened, about 7 minutes. Pour the syrup into a heatproof bowl, stir in the orange flower water, and set aside to cool to room temperature. Cover and refrigerate until well chilled, at least 2 hours. *At this point, the syrup may be refrigerated for up to 2 days.*

Slice the melon, cut off the rind, and cut the flesh into 2-cm (¾-in) cubes. In a serving bowl, combine the melon and grapes. Pour the chilled syrup over the fruit and toss gently to coat. *At this point, the salad can be refrigerated for up to 6 hours.*

Scatter with the pistachios and orange zest strips, and serve.

Barbeque party

This US deep south menu, designed for the sweltering days of summer, is a perfect choice for an celebration. It does require good weather!

Grilled Corn and Tomato Salad

Dry-Rubbed Ribs

Jicama Slaw with Chilli-Lime Dressing

Buttermilk Corn Bread

Minted Fruit Salad

Beer pairing: Belgian ale

Red-wine pairing: chilled Beaujolais nouveau

Set up a buffet for beer, wine, and soft drinks, filling galvanised tubs with ice and bottles. Choose local beers and soft drinks with colourful retro labels for a stylish tone.

Ahead of time

General party prep

Week of the party

- Assemble the necessary serving pieces:

  Serving bowls for corn and fruit salads and slaw

  Platter for ribs

  Basket or platter for corn bread

- Select music for party: Johnny Cash, Waylon Jennings, and Elvis Presley.
- Spruce up outdoor area where the party will take place, and make sure you have enough outdoor tables and chairs. This is a fun meal to serve family style at one long table. Arrange for tubs or other furnishings for the bar area.

Food and drink

Week of the party

- Stock up on beverages for the party. This is not an occasion for fine wines—the spicy flavours of the meal would drown their subtle flavours—but it is one when you can choose a range of beers, from Belgian ale to light and fruity local brews. Provide a crisp Sauvignon Blanc for the white-wine drinkers and pick up a Beaujolais nouveau, or other young red wine that is properly served chilled, to cover other tastes.
- Make dry rub for ribs.

Up to 2 days ahead

- Make a list and go grocery shopping.
- Make syrup for fruit salad.

Up to 1 day ahead

- Cut meat slabs into individual ribs and season with rub.
- Grill corn, let cool, and refrigerate.

Day of the party

Early in the day

- If serving buffet style, set up a buffet table in your outdoor space.
- If serving as a sit-down dinner, set the table. Alternatively, arrange seating around small tables to encourage conversation groups.
- Set up a bar area, complete with beer glasses, wineglasses, and bottle openers. Line beverage tubs with old white sheets, if desired, and assign a runner to pick up ice.

Up to 4 hours ahead

- Cut corn kernels from cobs.

Up to 3 hours ahead

- Bring ribs to room temperature and begin cooking.
- Make corn bread.
- Assemble slaw.

Up to 1 hour ahead

- Cut fruit for fruit salad.

Up to ½ hour ahead

- Chill white wine and Beaujolais nouveau in ice water. Fill beverage tubs with ice.
- Prepare grill for ribs and/or corn, if needed.
- Assemble corn salad.

Just before the party starts

- Assemble fruit salad.
- Warm corn bread.

After the party starts

During the party

- Keep an eye on the buffet and beverage table to keep them tidy.

As guests arrive

- Direct guests to the bar and offer potato chips and creamy dip.

During the party

- If your barbeque happens to be in celebration of a birthday, arrange for a piñata and let the guest of honour have the first whack at it.
- Complete your drink choices with some homemade iced tea garnished with plenty of mint.

Grilled Corn and Tomato Salad

preparation **45** minutes | cooking **20** minutes | **8–10** side-dish servings

This bright, crisp salad is a perfect foil for the spiciness of the ribs. If you like, grill the corn a day ahead, return it to the foil packets, and refrigerate overnight; let it come to room temperature before cutting the kernels from the cobs and assembling the salad.

tools | small saucepan | chef's knife | citrus reamer | kitchen shears | serrated utility knife | small mixing bowl | whisk | brush | grill or grill pan | wire grill brush (optional) | tongs

90 g (3 oz) unsalted butter, melted

3 drops of Tabasco sauce or pinch of ground cayenne pepper

2 Tbsp finely chopped fresh basil

1 tsp fine sea salt

½ tsp freshly ground black pepper

6 ears white or yellow corn, husks and silks removed

Extra-virgin olive oil for brushing, plus 125 ml (4 fl oz)

2 Tbsp fresh lime juice

2 Tbsp finely snipped fresh chives

1 bunch watercress, tough stems removed, separated into small sprigs

750 g (1½ lb) cherry tomatoes, halved through the stem end

In a small bowl, whisk together the melted butter, Tabasco, basil, ½ tsp of the salt, and ¼ tsp of the black pepper. Place 3 sheets of foil each 38 cm (15 in) long on a work surface, and place 2 ears of corn on each sheet. Brush the corn with the butter mixture. Wrap up snugly.

Prepare a fire in a charcoal grill or preheat a gas grill to medium. Scrape the rack clean with a wire brush, if necessary, and use paper towels to brush it lightly with olive oil. Position the grill rack or grill pan about 10 cm (4 in) from the heat source. (Alternatively, preheat a well-seasoned ridged stove-top grill pan.) Grill the corn packages for 10 minutes, turning occasionally with tongs. Unwrap the corn and grill the ears directly on the grill rack (or pan) for 5–10 minutes longer, turning to brown each side evenly. Watch the corn carefully; it should be nicely charred but not blackened. *At this point, the corn can be rewrapped in the foil and refrigerated up to overnight. Return to room temperature before proceeding.*

When the corn is cool enough to handle (or has returned to room temperature), place each ear over a large serving bowl and cut off the kernels, keeping the blade angled so you get the whole kernel but none of the tough cob. *At this point, the salad can be covered and refrigerated for up to 4 hours before finishing and serving. Return to room temperature for 20 minutes before finishing.*

Add the lime juice, 125 ml (4 fl oz) olive oil, chives, remaining ½ tsp salt, and remaining ¼ tsp black pepper to the bowl with the corn and toss to combine. Add the watercress and cherry tomatoes and toss gently. Serve at once.

Dry-Rubbed Ribs

preparation **10** minutes | marinating **2** hours | cooking **2¼** hours | **8–10** servings

In various parts of the South and the mid-Atlantic states, controversy rages over which are superior: wet or dry ribs. If you've never tried the dry version, you are in for a flavour revelation. While ribs can, of course, be barbequed over a low fire, the process is time-consuming and a little tricky. This method, which cooks the ribs in the oven and just finishes them on the grill for a hit of smoky flavour, is easier to pull off, especially when you have a gardenful of guests to attend to.

tools | very large mixing bowl | large lock-top plastic bags | 2 large roasting pans | grill (optional) | wire grill brush (optional) | tongs

FOR THE DRY RUB

60 g (2 oz) paprika

15 g (½ oz) freshly ground black pepper

60 g (2 oz) firmly packed dark brown sugar

3 Tbsp fine sea salt

4 tsp celery salt

4 tsp garlic powder

4 tsp dry mustard

4 tsp ground cumin

1½ tsp ground cayenne pepper

5 kg (10 lb) spare ribs (about 35 ribs when individually cut)

Vegetable oil for grill (optional)

In a very large bowl, stir together all the dry rub ingredients until thoroughly blended. *At this point, the rub can be stored at room temperature for up to 1 week in an airtight container.*

Add the ribs to the bowl of rub 5 at a time and rub the spices into them evenly on all sides. Transfer the ribs to large lock-top plastic bags, about 5 to a bag, letting the excess rub fall back into the bowl. Reserve excess rub for later use. Let stand at room temperature for at least 2 hours, or refrigerate for up to overnight. Return to room temperature before cooking.

Preheat the oven to 165°C (325°F). Divide the ribs between 2 very large roasting pans, placing them fatty side up. Bake until the meat is golden brown and no longer pink at the bone, 1½–1¾ hours. *At this point, the ribs can stand at room temperature for up to 1 hour before finishing on the grill.*

Prepare a fire in a charcoal grill, preheat a gas grill to medium-high, or preheat the grill. If using a charcoal or gas grill, scrape the rack clean with a wire brush, if necessary, and use paper towels to brush it lightly with oil. Position the grill rack or grill pan about 10 cm (4 in) from the heat source.

Sprinkle any remaining rub mixture over the cooked ribs and brown them briefly on the grill or under the grill, until sizzling.

At this point, the ribs can rest for up to 20 minutes before serving. The ribs may be served hot or warm.

sticky fingers Place a few containers of fancy wet wipes up and down the table for guests to clean their fingers after eating the ribs. Or, offer guests damp baby flannels, moistened with warm water from a kettle.

Jicama Slaw with Chilli-Lime Dressing

preparation **25** minutes | chilling **1** hour | **8–10** side-dish servings

Because it is so crisp and juicy, jicama slaw can take a spicy, citrusy dressing like the one here. In fact, all across Mexico slices of cold, peeled jicama are sold as roadside snacks. The only garnish? A drizzle of fresh lime juice and a dusting of hot chilli powder.

tools | citrus reamer | salad spinner (optional) | chef's knife | vegetable peeler | box grater | large mixing bowl | whisk | 2 wooden spoons

750 g (1½ lb) jicama

375 g (¾ lb) carrots

30 g (1 oz) loosely packed fresh coriander leaves

1 jalapeño chilli

60 ml (2 fl oz) fresh lime juice

60 g (2 oz) sour cream

60 ml (2 fl oz) mayonnaise, homemade if desired (below)

1 tsp fine sea salt

½ tsp chilli powder

Pale inner leaves from 1 large head romaine (cos) lettuce (8–10 leaves), spun dry (optional)

With a vegetable peeler, peel the jicama and the carrots. Use the largest holes of a box grater to coarsely shred both.

Finely chop the coriander leaves. Halve, seed, and chop the chilli.

In a large glass or ceramic bowl, combine the lime juice, sour cream, mayonnaise, salt, chilli powder, jalapeño, and coriander and whisk together. Add the jicama and carrot and toss to mix. Cover and refrigerate for at least 1 hour to allow the flavours to blend. *At this point, the slaw can be refrigerated for up to 3 hours.*

Take the salad from the refrigerator just before serving. Toss again to distribute the dressing. Scoop some salad into each lettuce leaf, if desired, and serve.

homemade mayonnaise It's a little extra work, but once you've tried it you may never go back to shop-bought. Warm 1 large uncracked egg in a bowl of hot tap water for 3 minutes. In a blender or food processor, combine the egg, 1 tsp Dijon mustard, 1 tsp fresh lemon juice or white wine vinegar, ½ tsp salt, and ¼ tsp pepper. In a glass measuring jug, combine 180 ml (6 fl oz) olive oil and the same amount of grapeseed oil. With the motor running, slowly drizzle the combined oils into the blender (so slowly that it should take at least 1 minute) to make a thick sauce. Stir in 1 Tbsp hot water. Makes about 430 ml (14 fl oz) mayonnaise.

Buttermilk Corn Bread

preparation **30** minutes | cooking **15** minutes | cooling **10** minutes | **8–10** side-dish servings

For the best results, use medium-grind stone-ground cornmeal. If serving the corn bread warm, offer tubs of whipped butter seasoned with chilli powder for spreading.

tools | small saucepan | chef's knife | muffin pan | mixing bowl | chef's knife | whisk | rack

185 g (6 oz) cornmeal

155 g (5 oz) flour

2 Tbsp sugar

2 tsp baking powder

Fine sea salt and black pepper

1 large egg, lightly beaten

250 ml (8 fl oz) buttermilk

6 Tbsp (90 g /3 oz) butter, melted

185 g (6 oz) corn kernels

⅛ tsp ground cayenne pepper

Preheat the oven to 220°C (425°F). Butter a standard 12-cup cake tin or a 3-litre (3-qt) baking dish.

In a large mixing bowl, stir together the cornmeal, flour, sugar, baking powder, 1 tsp salt, and ½ tsp pepper. Make a well in the centre of the mixture and add the egg, buttermilk, melted butter, corn, and cayenne. Using a fork to whisk from the centre, blend the ingredients into a loose and lumpy batter; do not overmix.

Pour the batter into the prepared muffin cups or dish and bake until lightly browned and pulling away from the sides of the pan, about 15 minutes for a cake tin, 25 minutes for a baking dish. Transfer to a wire rack and let cool for 10 minutes. Turn the breads out of the pan or cut into squares. *At this point, the corn bread can be held for up to 3 hours.* Serve warm or at room temperature.

Minted Fruit Salad

preparation **45** minutes | cooking **10** minutes | chilling **2** hours | **8–10** dessert servings

Use a mixture of strawberries and blueberries for a brightly coloured salad. To save time, look for precut pineapple and light syrup–packed mango spears in glass jars.

tools | citrus reamer | saucepan | chef's knife | mixing bowl

310 ml (10 fl oz) simple syrup (page 176)

3 Tbsp fresh lime juice

1 large papaya, about 1 kg (2 lb)

1 mango

750 g (1½ lb) berries

375 g (¾ lb) cut pineapple

15 g (½ oz) mint leaves

1 Tbsp dark rum (optional)

Put the syrup in a saucepan over low heat. Cover and bring just to a simmer. Pour into a heatproof bowl, stir in the lime juice, and set aside to cool to room temperature. Cover and refrigerate until well chilled, at least 2 hours.

Prepare the fruits for the salad. Peel and seed the papaya and cut it into 2.5-cm (1-in) chunks. Peel and pit the mango, and cut it into 2.5-cm (1-in) chunks. Hull and halve strawberries, if using. Coarsely chop the mint, setting aside a few nice leaves for garnish. In a large glass or ceramic bowl, combine all the fruits and toss to mix. Drizzle with the syrup, scatter with the chopped mint, and toss very gently. If desired, drizzle with the rum. Garnish with the mint leaves and serve.

Asian grill

The bright and sprightly flavours in this simple menu are the perfect pick-me-up after a day at the office. Your guests will forget all cares as they dip their spring rolls.

Sesame Noodles

Vietnamese Spring Rolls

Nuoc Cham Dipping Sauce

Peanut Dipping Sauce

Ginger-Soy Chicken Thighs

White-wine pairing: Grüner Veltliner or sake

Rosé pairing: Bandol

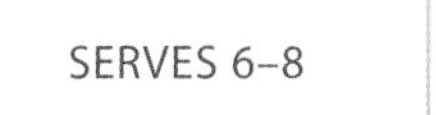

Hang silk or paper lanterns, and place glowing tea lights all around. Decorate with bonsai and hand out Asian fans for guests to keep themselves cool. Use only chopsticks for eating.

Ahead of time

General party prep

Week of the party

- Assemble the necessary serving pieces:

  Large, shallow serving bowl for sesame noodles

  Large serving platter for spring rolls

  Platter for chicken kebabs

  Square bamboo or etched glass cups for sake

  Dessert bowls and spoons for sorbet, if serving

- Spruce up outdoor area where the party will take place, making sure you have enough outdoor tables and chairs. Serve this casual menu as a stand-up buffet, a sit-down dinner, or something in between: provide seating and place rolled, cutlery-filled napkins on one of the tables, letting guests find their own seats around the outdoor dining area.

Food and drink

Week of the party

- Stock up on drink for the party. Choose a crisp, dry white wine, such as a Grüner Veltliner or a sauvignon blanc; a flavourful, dry rosé, such as Bandol; and/or good-quality sake. Offer a selection of Thai and Chinese beers, and perhaps some iced, exotically flavoured green tea.

Up to 2 days ahead

- Make a list and go grocery shopping.
- Make *nuoc cham* dipping sauce.
- Make peanut dipping sauce.

Day of the party	After the party starts
Early in the day ■ Set up your outdoor space. Place the grill off to one side, and assemble the bar area and the platter and bowls for the spring rolls, with their dipping sauces, on the opposite side of the deck, patio, or garden. ■ If serving as a sit-down dinner, set the table. Alternatively, arrange seating around small tables to encourage conversation groups.	**During the party** ■ Pass out little red good-luck envelopes to your guests with thoughtful fortunes or party dares, such as singing a solo or making a toast. (Your party's invitations could echo this theme of red envelopes.)
Up to 4 hours ahead ■ The spouse who gets home from work first marinates chicken. ■ And cooks noodles and tosses with oil. ■ And makes spring roll prawn filling, then refrigerates. **Up to 2 hours ahead** ■ Spouse number 2 assembles spring rolls while spouse number 1 puts his or her feet up. ■ A coin toss decides who soaks skewers for chicken. **Up to ½ hour ahead** ■ Chill white wine, rosé, and sake in ice water. ■ Prepare grill.	**As guests arrive** ■ One host grills the chicken, while the other garnishes the peanut sauce and cuts and serves spring rolls. **During the party** ■ Complement the menu with broccoli slaw or another ready-made bagged slaw tossed with balsamic-soy vinaigrette. **At the end of the evening** ■ Finish the evening with a selection of sorbets in tropical flavours, such as mango, coconut, and pineapple.

Sesame Noodles

preparation **30** minutes | cooking **15** minutes | chilling **30** minutes | **6–8** small-plate servings

This classic dish seems to appeal to virtually everyone. It also makes a nice main course for a light lunch, accompanied by a salad of spicy baby greens and glasses of iced green tea.

tools | vegetable peeler | chef's knife | citrus reamer | small frying pan | large pot | colander | blender

500 g (1 lb) soba noodles or angel hair pasta

2 Tbsp Asian sesame oil

2 Tbsp peanut oil

2.5-cm (1-in) knob fresh ginger, peeled and minced

3 cloves garlic, chopped

1½ tsp red chilli paste

Juice of 1 large lime

75 g (2½ oz) creamy peanut butter

60 ml (2 fl oz) unseasoned rice vinegar

2 Tbsp brown sugar

3 Tbsp low-sodium soy sauce

60 ml (2 fl oz) hot water

1 red pepper (capsicum), seeded and cut into small dice

1 Tbsp sesame seeds, lightly toasted (right)

Chopped fresh coriander for garnish

Chopped salted roasted peanuts for garnish

Bring a large pot of unsalted water to the boil. Add the noodles and cook, stirring to break up any clumps, just until tender but still firm, according to the package directions. Drain immediately and rinse thoroughly with cold water. Drain the noodles well again and transfer to a large, shallow serving bowl. Immediately drizzle with the sesame oil and toss to coat well, so the noodles won't stick together. Cover and refrigerate for at least 30 minutes to let the noodles absorb the sesame oil flavour.

In a blender or a food processor, combine the peanut oil, ginger, garlic, chilli paste, lime juice, peanut butter, vinegar, brown sugar, soy sauce, and hot water and process to make a smooth sauce. Toss the noodles with the sauce. *At this point, the noodles can be held for 30 minutes at room temperature or refrigerated for up to 4 hours.*

When ready to serve, toss the noodles with about three-quarters of the diced pepper. Garnish with the remaining bell pepper, the sesame seeds, the coriander, and the peanuts. Serve cold or at cool room temperature.

toasted seeds and nuts To toast sesame seeds for this recipe, place a small, dry frying pan over medium heat, add the sesame seeds, and toast, shaking the pan often, until the seeds are pale golden brown, about 3 minutes. Pour onto a plate to cool. The same technique with a longer time frame may be used for nuts such as pecans and almonds; simply toast until golden brown and fragrant.

Vietnamese Spring Rolls

preparation **1** hour | cooking **6** minutes | cooling **20** minutes | **6–8** small-plate servings

To distinguish them from their crunchy deep-fried counterparts of the same name, these rice paper–wrapped packages are known as "fresh" spring rolls. Although the rice paper may seem too brittle to fold, just a few moments in warm water renders it pliable. If desired, substitute 12-mm (½-in) matchsticks of firm tofu, fried in peanut oil until just golden, for the prawns in the filling.

tools | vegetable peeler | chef's knife | paring knife | small mixing bowl | citrus reamer | frying pan | medium mixing bowl | large, shallow bowl | kitchen towel | serrated utility knife

1 Tbsp peanut oil

2 tsp peeled and finely chopped fresh ginger

2 cloves garlic, finely chopped

375 g (¾ lb) peeled and deveined medium prawns, halved lengthwise

Dash of salt

1½ tsp Asian chilli sauce

1 tsp Asian sesame oil

2 ripe avocados

6 spring onions, pale and dark green parts, thinly sliced

2 Tbsp fresh mint chiffonade (page 101)

2 Tbsp fresh basil chiffonade

12 rice paper rounds, 20–30 cm (8–12 in) in diameter

12 butter lettuce leaves, centre ribs discarded, torn into 7.5-cm (3-in) pieces

Nuoc cham dipping sauce (opposite)

Peanut dipping sauce (opposite)

Place a frying pan over medium-high heat and add the peanut oil. When it is hot, add the ginger and garlic and stir for 30 seconds. Add the prawns and season with salt. Cook until the prawns just begin to curl, about 1 minute. Stir in the chilli sauce and sesame oil and remove from the heat. Let cool to room temperature before filling the rolls. *At this point, the prawn mixture can be transferred to a bowl, covered, and refrigerated for up to 4 hours.*

Halve, stone, and peel the avocados, then cut into small pieces. In a medium bowl, stir together the prawn mixture, avocados, spring onions, mint, and basil.

Have ready on a work surface: a large, shallow bowl filled with warm water, a damp kitchen towel, the rice paper rounds, the lettuce, and the prawn mixture. Immerse a rice paper round in the water for 2–3 seconds, then remove and spread on the towel. Place a few pieces of lettuce along the centre line of the rice paper, leaving 2.5–5 cm (1–2 in) uncovered on either side. Spread about 1 heaped Tbsp of the filling in a line along the lettuce. Fold the bottom half of the rice paper up and over to cover the filling, tucking it under the far edge of the filling and compacting it gently but firmly. Fold in the left and right sides of the rice paper and continue rolling up toward the top edge, again compacting gently but firmly, to the end, forming a tight cylinder. Place the spring roll, seam side down, on a large platter. Repeat with the remaining ingredients until you have made about 12 rolls. Cover the rolls with the damp towel and set them aside until serving time, not more than 2 hours.

To serve, use a sharp serrated knife to cut each roll in half. Arrange on a large serving platter. Transfer the dipping sauces to small serving bowls and place on either end of the serving platter or alongside the platter.

Nuoc Cham Dipping Sauce

preparation **10** minutes | standing **30** minutes | makes about **180** ml (**6** fl oz)

This popular dipping sauce is ubiquitous on Vietnamese tables.

tools | chef's knife | citrus reamer | small mixing bowl

In a small bowl, combine lime juice, sugar, fish sauce, rice vinegar, coriander, and garlic. Stir until the sugar dissolves. Let stand at room temperature for at least 30 minutes. *At this point, the sauce can be covered and refrigerated for up to 2 days. Bring to room temperature before serving.*

> **fish sauce** A very popular seasoning throughout Southeast Asia, fish sauce adds a salty, savoury flavour to all kinds of dishes. Vietnamese fish sauce is called *nuoc mam,* while Thai fish sauce is known as *nam pla.* Either may be used here.

125 ml (4 fl oz) fresh lime juice

60 g (2 oz) sugar

3 Tbsp Vietnamese or Thai fish sauce

1 Tbsp unseasoned rice vinegar

1 Tbsp chopped fresh coriander

2 cloves garlic, chopped

Peanut Dipping Sauce

preparation **10** minutes | cooking **5** minutes | makes about **250** ml (**8** fl oz)

This savoury dipping sauce complements almost any type of grilled meat, such as the beef satay on page 53.

tools | chef's knife | small saucepan | whisk

Pour the peanut oil into a small saucepan over medium heat. When the oil is hot, add the garlic and stir just until the garlic begins to take on colour, less than 1 minute. Add the chicken stock, hoisin sauce, peanut butter, chilli paste, tomato paste, and sugar. Whisk until smooth, bring to a simmer, and cook, stirring, for about 3 minutes to blend the flavours. Remove from the heat and set aside to cool to room temperature. *At this point, the sauce may be covered and refrigerated for up to 2 days. Bring to room temperature before serving.* Sprinkle the dipping sauce with roasted peanuts just before serving.

1 Tbsp peanut oil

2 cloves garlic, chopped

160 ml (5 fl oz) chicken stock

60 ml (2 fl oz) hoisin sauce

2 Tbsp creamy peanut butter

1 tsp Asian chilli paste

1 tsp tomato paste

½ tsp sugar

60 g (2 oz) finely chopped roasted peanuts

Ginger-Soy Chicken Thighs

preparation **25** minutes | marinating **30** minutes | cooking **10** minutes | **6–8** servings

The ginger lends an unexpected sweet tang to these tasty, succulent chicken kebabs. If ginger preserve is unavailable, substitute the same quantity of lemon or orange marmalade with the addition of 1 Tbsp peeled and minced fresh ginger.

tools | chef's knife | citrus reamer | mixing bowl | whisk | baking dish | 12–16 bamboo skewers | grill | wire grill brush (optional) | tongs

12–16 boneless, skinless chicken thighs

155 g (5 oz) ginger preserve

60 g (2 oz) minced shallot

90 ml (3 fl oz) fresh lemon juice

60 ml (2 fl oz) extra-virgin olive oil, plus extra for brushing

60 ml (2 fl oz) low-sodium soy sauce

8 spring onions, white and pale green parts, minced

Pat the chicken thighs dry thoroughly with paper towels. In a bowl, whisk together the ginger preserve, shallot, lemon juice, olive oil, and soy sauce. Reserve half of the ginger mixture for serving and transfer the rest to a large, shallow ceramic or glass baking dish to use as a marinade. Add the thighs and half of the spring onions and turn to coat generously on all sides with the marinade. Set aside, covered, at room temperature while the grill heats, about 30 minutes. *At this point, you can refrigerate the chicken for up to 4 hours; bring back to room temperature before grilling.* Meanwhile, soak the skewers in water to cover for at least 30 minutes.

Prepare a fire in a charcoal grill or preheat a gas grill to medium-high. Scrape the rack clean with a wire brush, if necessary, and use paper towels to brush it lightly with olive oil. Position the grill rack about 10 cm (4 in) from the heat source.

Drain the skewers. Place a chicken thigh, spread out flat, on a work surface with the long side facing you. Skewer with 2 skewers, with the points facing away from you, the first about 2.5 cm (1 in) in from the short left side of the thigh and the second about the same distance in from the short right side of the thigh. Add a second thigh to the 2 skewers in the same way. To ensure that the thighs lie flat and cook evenly and quickly, put the meaty side on the left with the first thigh, then on the right with the second thigh, to balance the weight, and leave a gap between the thighs for heat and air circulation while grilling. Repeat with the remaining thighs and skewers so each pair of skewers holds 2 thighs.

Arrange the assembled kebabs on the rack and grill, turning once, until the thighs are golden and firm, about 5 minutes per side. (Move the kebabs to a cooler area after the first minute if the coals flare up or the kebabs are in danger of charring.) Transfer to a platter and drizzle generously with the reserved ginger-soy mixture (*not* the marinade). Scatter with the remaining green onions and serve. Direct guests to push the chicken off of the stewers before eating.

Michael

Mellisa

Lillian

SPECIAL OCCASIONS

Holidays and milestones such as birthdays, arrivals of babies, engagements, and anniversaries are wonderful times to share good food and make future memories with your old and new friends and family.

As a newly created family, you can share your joy with others throughout the year by offering to host special events. The menus in this chapter are versatile enough to work as an engagement dinner or a Christmas dinner, a baby shower brunch or a brunch celebrating the arrival of a good friend into town. And, if you're wondering how to juggle competing claims on your holiday time by two sets of in-laws, here's a simple solution: start a new tradition and ask all of them to come to you. No one could refuse such a gracious request from a pair of happy newlyweds.

Making occasions special

The menus in this chapter are designed as holiday dinners or parties honouring important guests or events, but any party in this book can be transformed into a special occasion with just a few changes.

First, special occasions call for a more formal approach to the invitations and table settings. Sending paper invitations helps build anticipation, and guests are likely to treat them more seriously than a casual mention by e-mail or phone. The style of the invitations can be carried over to the place cards, another key element in a special occasion. A table set with place cards makes guests feel welcome and looked after, and minimizes the initial confusion that sometimes results when guests are not shown where to sit. It also helps you enforce a seating arrangement that you think will lead to the best conversations, a thoughtful gesture on the hosts' part.

Planning and extras

Holidays, engagement parties, and dinners honouring one or more guests call for some advance thought and planning to be truly memorable. At least four to six weeks in advance, begin to brainstorm ideas that will make the gathering unique. For example, you might decide to display old family photographs, ask close friends to make toasts or do readings, or even show a short video prepared by a family member or good friend. Such ideas require the help of others, so you'll need to allow everyone plenty of time to prepare. For a birthday, you might decide to play music that corresponds to the guest of honour's date of birth, and include a line on the invitation to dress in the fashions of the era. For an engagement party, it is nice to provide an individual touch. Design of your own wine label to paste on the reverse side of the wine bottle provides a wonderful memory for all.

For a large or important event, it is often a good idea to hire a helper—either a bartender to make drinks and free up one host for other duties, or a server who can assist with clearing surfaces at a cocktail party or with serving, clearing the table, and washing up after a sit-down dinner. Caterers often have phone numbers of waiters who regularly seek one-time-only jobs to fill openings in their schedule. You'll thank yourselves for lightening the workload.

A FORMAL TABLE

A formal table calls for a tablecloth, classically of white damask, a fine cloth made of linen, silk, or other fibres that features an intricate design (usually flowers or fruit) created during the weaving process. Always place a pad on the table before topping it with the cloth, to prevent slippage. The middle crease should run in a straight line lengthwise down the centre of the table, and the drop from each side of the table should be about 45 cm (18 in).

Any dining table benefits from the presence of flowers, but a formal table can also show off your finest decorative pieces. If you have an old-fashioned silver candelabra, entwine it with dainty vining flowers, such as clematis. Or, float candles, interspersed with camellia blossoms, rose petals, or citrus slices, in a wide, shallow crystal bowl.

CHAMPAGNE DREAMS

A glass of bubbly is a clear signal that your event is a special one. Champagne creates an excitement unlike any other wine. It comes in a number of styles, from the driest brut to the sweetest doux. It may be made from white Chardonnay grapes (*blanc de blancs*, or "white from white grapes") or from black Pinot Noir grapes (*blanc de noirs*, "white from black grapes"), or it can be a rosé. You can choose a classic Champagne from the region of the same name in France, or a premium sparkling wine from elsewhere in the world.

While old-fashioned champagne saucers have a nostalgic appeal, they don't show off sparkling wine to best advantage because their shape allows the bubbles to disappear too quickly. Tall, slender flutes, with their tapered shape designed to trap bubbles, help prolong the sparkling wine's signature effervescence.

Michael

Celebrating holidays

Now that you are married, you are setting out on a wonderful adventure: creating the holiday traditions that will help define your new family. If you'd like to host a holiday meal in your own home, a menu in this chapter will help you tackle that challenge with grace. Decide together the best way to proceed for the important holidays, to avoid misunderstandings. Will you open presents on Christmas Eve or Christmas Day? Will you ask an older family member to carve the turkey, or will you or your spouse assume that responsibility? (If you decide to do it, you might want to practice with a roast chicken beforehand!) How will you graciously handle the blending of your two families? Are there special requirements, such as dietary restrictions, that must be kept in mind? Put your best diplomatic foot forward to find a way to satisfy everyone's expectations, while making sure that your own are respected, too. If you have fun at a holiday celebration, everyone else will too.

SPECIAL TOUCHES

Holiday celebrations offer the perfect opportunity to add extra flourishes. These can be decorative details, such as a miniature bouquet of holiday greens and berries tied to the back of each chair, or a take-home seasonal offering, such as a jar of homemade marmalade or a tin of cookies. When children are present, consider putting a small gift at each place setting or making a special holiday beverage—perhaps hot chocolate with a peppermint swizzle stick—just for them.

Use floor and table lamps and groups of candles to create soft, flattering pools of light. Dim or turn off overhead lights. A strand of small white lights strung along a banister or the edge of a mantelpiece creates a holiday sparkle and adds to the festive spirit.

Family time

Holiday events typically include children: your nieces and nephews, younger siblings, or perhaps, in time, your own kids. Plan ahead for keeping youngsters entertained by renting movies, stocking a few board games, and providing a spill-over space for kids to play and wrestle in. This will ensure that the grown-ups have the necessary physical and psychological space in which to chat about holidays past and to gossip about absent relatives without having to shout to be heard. And don't hesitate to put older children to work in the kitchen. It's good for them, and they'll enjoy it.

Putting on the full holiday meal alone is not only difficult, but also unnecessary. It may also sour you on hosting future celebrations! Keep an open mind to offers of help from in-laws, even if the dish your spouse's aunt suggests does not fit in with your carefully planned menu. Accept the offer graciously—you'll reap the rewards for years to come. Asking the bakers to bring dessert is not only a help to you, but a thoughtful way to make them feel involved with a meal that they, perhaps, have piloted for many years. You should also recruit the parents to make a toast or say a blessing before the meal begins, for the same reason.

GIFT-GIVING TRADITIONS

When guests are invited for a holiday that involves gift giving, you can take charge and declare the rules, preventing any confusion and also increasing the fun.

Many families enjoy "secret Santa" or "white elephant" gift exchanges. For the latter, each guest (and host) brings a wrapped gift and sets it in a pile—perhaps an amusing item or a hopelessly tacky one, found in the attic or purchased for a modest amount (be sure to set a reasonable limit on expense). Players draw numbers and, starting with the lowest number, select a gift to unwrap or claim a previously opened gift from its owner. The player who went first gets another chance to claim another's gift at the end, and then a vote is taken to determine the best and worst gifts. Sometimes these two gifts must be swapped. Add your own rules and invent a new tradition!

Harvest dinner

This menu features all the bounty of the autumn season, from squash soup to a nut tart, and does double duty as a holiday feast that honours both tradition and innovation.

Squash Soup with Thyme Cream

Fresh Cranberry-Ginger Relish

Lemon and Sage Turkey

Rich Port Gravy

Buttermilk Mashed Potatoes

Braised Chard with Garlic

Pecan Tart

White-wine pairing: white Burgundy
Red-wine pairing: old-vine Zinfandel

SERVES 8–10

Be warned: The turkey in this menu, dry-brined for days to create crisp skin and juicy meat, is so delicious that you may find yourself nominated to cook it for the family every year.

Ahead of time

General party prep

Week of the party

- Assemble the necessary serving pieces:

  Platter for turkey

  Sauceboat or small jug for gravy

  Serving bowls for chard, potatoes, relish

- Plan decorations with flowers, candles, seasonal fruit.
- Clean and decorate the house.
- Producing a feast like this is manageable if you are organized. Using this workplan as a guide, write up your own list of tasks; add one spouse's initials after each entry, then copy the list so you each have one.

Food and drink

Week of the party

- Visit a wine merchant to select the bottles you need. Offer a white Burgundy from France or a good buttery Chardonnay from California. For red-wine drinkers, choose an old-vine Zinfandel with rich berry flavours.
- Make sure you stock up with plenty of sparkling water and healthful sodas, plus sparkling apple juice or ginger beer.
- Call the butcher to reserve a turkey.
- Make cranberry relish and refrigerate.
- Make pastry for tart, bake blind, and freeze.

Up to 3 days ahead

- Make a list and go grocery shopping.
- Dry-brine turkey.
- Start port gravy.

Up to 1 day ahead

- Roast squash and make thyme cream for soup.
- Make pecan tart and refrigerate.

Day of the party

Early in the day

- Place wine and all other beverages on a separate buffet table to prevent traffic jams. Use a worktable or desk covered with a coloured underskirt and festive seasonal tablecloth.
- Set the table.
- Determine the seating order and make place cards.
- Set up post-dinner coffee service.

6 hours ahead

- Bring turkey to room temperature.
- Make squash soup up to, but not including, cream.

4 hours ahead

- Preheat oven and begin cooking turkey.

Up to 2 hours ahead

- Trim and slice chard and slice garlic for chard.
- Peel potatoes and let stand in water.

Up to ½ hour ahead

- Cook potatoes and hold, covered, at room temperature.
- Cook chard and hold, covered, at room temperature or on a warming tray.
- Rewarm soup and add cream.
- Chill white wine in ice water.

After the party starts

As guests arrive

- One spouse takes coats while the other offers sparkling cider and nuts as appetizers.
- Choose a willing relative or friend to take responsibility for clearing the soup bowls and spoons after the first course so that you will be free to concentrate on the gravy and potatoes.

After guests arrive

- Remove the turkey from the oven and let rest.
- Finish gravy and hold in the top of a double boiler.
- Finish mashed potatoes. If you like, assign this task to a family member.
- Bring pecan tart to room temperature.
- As you sit down for soup, put dinner plates in the (turned-off) oven to warm, then bring them to the table with oven mitts while the turkey is being carved.

After dinner

- When it comes time to clear, one spouse can scrape and carefully stack plates while the other concentrates on dessert and coffee.
- Make bourbon whipped cream, if desired.
- At coffee time, offer hot apple cider with orange zest strips and star anise.

Squash Soup with Thyme Cream

preparation **25** minutes | cooking **1¼** hours | **8–10** first-course servings

The thyme adds an earthy flavour note to this creamy and comforting golden soup. Place wide, shallow soup bowls atop chargers or dinner plates so the table will not look empty between the soup course and the arrival of the turkey.

tools | chef's knife | large, rimmed baking sheet | small bowl | whisk |2 large saucepans | large metal spoon | blender | fine-mesh sieve | ladle

125 g (4 oz) crème fraîche or sour cream

1 tsp minced fresh thyme

Salt and ground white pepper

2 large winter squash such as butternut, 1.75–2 kg (3½–4 lb) total weight, halved and seeded

6 Tbsp (90 g/3 oz) unsalted butter

1 onion, chopped

1.25 litres (40 fl oz) chicken stock

250 ml (8 fl oz) double cream

Preheat the oven to 180°C (350°F). Line a large, rimmed baking sheet with aluminum foil. In a small bowl, whisk together the crème fraîche, thyme, and ⅛ tsp white pepper. Cover and refrigerate until serving time. *At this point, the thyme cream can be refrigerated for up to 1 day.*

Place the squash halves, cut side up, on the prepared baking sheet. Put 1 Tbsp of the butter in each squash cavity and season the squash with salt and pepper. Roast until tender, about 45 minutes. *At this point, the squash can be refrigerated for up to 1 day. Bring it back to room temperature before proceeding.*

Melt the remaining 2 Tbsp butter in a large saucepan over low heat. Add the onion and cook, stirring occasionally, until softened but not brown, about 5 minutes. Scoop the squash flesh out of the skins into the saucepan, then add the stock and stir until smooth. Bring to a simmer over medium heat. Cook, stirring occasionally, until reduced by about one-fourth, about 30 minutes.

Remove from the heat and let cool, uncovered, for about 5 minutes. Working in batches if necessary, purée the soup in a blender or food processor or with a stick blender until completely smooth. (If using a blender, be sure to hold the top on firmly when blending hot liquids.) *At this point, the soup can stand for up to 1 hour at room temperature or be covered and refrigerated for up to 6 hours.*

Strain the soup through a fine-mesh sieve into a clean saucepan and stir in the cream, 1½ tsp salt, and a pinch of white pepper. Rewarm the soup over low heat; taste and adjust the seasoning.

Ladle into bowls and gently swirl about 1½ tsp of the thyme cream into the centre of each serving. Serve at once.

seasonal decorations Create a cornucopia centrepiece overflowing with grapes, apples, oranges, and pears. Scatter fresh or faux fall leaves found at a crafts store.

Fresh Cranberry-Ginger Relish

preparation **20** minutes | chilling **4** minutes | **8–10** first-course servings

This unexpected uncooked relish could not be easier to make, and the tart-sweet ginger flavour is a nice counterpoint to the rich turkey and earthy sides of the meal. When first blended, the sugar will seem granular and gritty, but it quickly dissolves in the cranberry juices to make a bright, jewel-coloured syrup. Use dry-packed candied ginger for this surprisingly delicious relish, not ginger preserves from a jar.

tools | chef's knife | citrus zester | food processor

1 bag (12 oz/375 g) fresh cranberries

1 lemon, scrubbed under hot water to remove any wax

155 g (5 oz) sugar

90 g (3 oz) crystallised ginger, coarsely chopped

¼ tsp ground ginger

Rinse and drain the cranberries. Pick over and discard any bruised or soft ones. Spread in a single layer on a double layer of paper towels; place 2 more layers of paper towels on the top and gently pat the berries dry.

Remove the zest from lemon in thin strips and chop coarsely. Save the rest of the lemon for another use.

In a food processor, pulse the cranberries, lemon zest, sugar, candied ginger, and ground ginger just until finely chopped. Cover and refrigerate for at least 4 hours and preferably 24 hours before serving. *If desired, the relish can be stored for up to 1 week in the refrigerator.*

crystallised ginger You can buy crystallised, ginger—or make it yourself at home, to use in this relish, to use as a cocktail garnish, or to give away during the holidays. Bring 375 ml (12 fl oz) water to the boil. Stir in 125 g (4 oz) sugar until dissolved. Cook over medium heat for 5 minutes, then add 125 g (4 oz) thinly sliced (3 mm / ⅛ in), peeled fresh ginger. Reduce the heat to a simmer and cook until tender, about 10 minutes. Drain, then put the ginger in a bowl with 125 g (4 oz) sugar and toss to coat. Spread out in a single layer on waxed paper and let cool. Store in a tightly covered jar for up to 3 weeks.

Lemon and Sage Turkey

preparation **30** minutes | brining **3** days | standing **1** hour | cooking **3** hours | **10** servings

In recent years, brining, as well as shorter cooking times and the liberal use of herbs, have revolutionised the holiday bird. The process of dry-brining detailed here lends the same delectably succulent flavour to the meat as wet-brining, but has the added advantage of yielding a crisp, golden skin.

tools | small saucepan | chef's knife | large roasting rack | large roasting pan | brush | kitchen string | instant-read thermometer | carving set

1 fresh turkey, 6–7 kg (12–14 lb), preferably organic

8 small sprigs fresh sage

Coarse sea salt and freshly ground pepper

2 Tbsp unsalted butter, melted

3 lemons, preferably organic, scrubbed and quartered

Three days before you plan to serve the turkey, pull out the neck and the giblets to use for the Rich Port Gravy (page 144). Discard the kidney(s), if they are included.

Rinse the turkey inside and out with cold water and pat dry with plenty of paper towels. Don't rush; be sure it's really dry all over. Gently slide two fingers under the skin of each breast and push 2 of the sage sprigs under the skin on each side. Do the same over the plumpest part of each thigh. Be careful not to tear or puncture the skin. Measure out ¾ tsp salt for each 500-g (1-lb) of turkey (for example, approximately 9 tsp, or 3 Tbsp, for a 6-kg/12-lb turkey). Place the turkey on a rack over a roasting pan and distribute the salt over the entire turkey, concentrating the salt over the thicker parts of the breasts and thighs. Place the uncovered turkey in the refrigerator.

On the day of serving, remove the turkey from the refrigerator and again dry very thoroughly inside and out with plenty of paper towels. Let stand for 1 hour to come to room temperature and dry out the skin slightly. While the turkey sits, preheat the oven to 190°C (375°F).

Brush the skin with the melted butter and season with pepper. Place the lemon quarters inside the cavity and tie the legs together. Place the turkey in the oven with the legs toward the rear and roast for 45 minutes, until the breast has begun to brown. Reduce the oven temperature to 120°C (250°F), add 1 Tbsp of water to the bottom of the roasting pan, and cover the bird loosely with foil. Roast for 2½–3 hours, approximately 29 minutes per kilogram, or until an instant-read thermometer inserted into the turkey at the thickest part of the breast registers 68°–71°C (155°–160°F). Baste with the pan juices every 30 minutes.

When the turkey is done, remove it from the oven and let stand, loosely covered with the foil, for 30 minutes. Carve the turkey and serve the gravy on the side.

Rich Port Gravy

preparation **25** minutes | cooking **1¾** hours | **8–10** servings

If poultry is to the cook what canvas is to the painter, this velvety gravy is the equivalent of rich-hued oil paints. It provides the perfect counterpoint to the moist, golden bird that results from the recipe on page 142, and it can be prepared in advance to help keep the holiday kitchen calm. Get a head start on the gravy when you start brining the bird.

tools | chef's knife | vegetable peeler | 2 large saucepans | wooden spoon | metal spoon | fine-mesh sieve | glass measuring jug | sauce whisk | double boiler (optional)

Neck and giblets reserved from fresh turkey (page 142)

1 carrot

1 onion

1 stalk celery

1 head garlic

5 Tbsp (75 g /2½ oz) unsalted butter

1 Tbsp rapeseed oil

1 sprig fresh thyme

250 ml (8 fl oz) dry white wine

500 ml (16 fl oz) ruby port

1 litre (32 fl oz) chicken stock

45 g (1½ oz) flour

180 ml (6 fl oz) double cream

One to three days before you plan to serve the Lemon and Sage Turkey (page 142), begin the gravy. Coarsely chop the reserved turkey neck and giblets. Peel and coarsely chop the carrot. Coarsely chop the onion and celery. Remove the loose papery skin from the garlic and cut the head in half crosswise.

Heat 1 Tbsp of the butter and the oil in a large saucepan over high heat until the butter melts. Add the turkey neck and giblets, carrot, onion, and celery and cook, stirring often, until all the ingredients are dark golden brown but not scorched, 8–10 minutes. Add the halved head of garlic, thyme, white wine, and port and use a wooden spoon to deglaze the pan, stirring and scraping up all the browned bits from the pan bottom. Add the chicken stock, bring to the boil, and reduce the heat to maintain a simmer. Let the mixture cook, uncovered, until slightly reduced and very flavourful, about 1½ hours, skimming foam and grease from the surface of the gravy every 20 minutes with a large, shallow metal spoon.

Strain the stock through a fine-mesh sieve into a large saucepan, pressing down on the solids with the back of a spoon. Place over medium-high heat and simmer briskly until reduced by about half, degreasing again if necessary. Transfer to a glass container to help the liquid cool faster, then cool, cover, and refrigerate overnight. *At this point, the reduced stock can be refrigerated for up to 3 days.*

On the day of serving, while the turkey roasts, finish the gravy: In a large, clean saucepan, melt the remaining 4 Tbsp (60 g / 2 oz) butter over medium-low heat and stir in the flour. Cook, stirring constantly with a sauce whisk, until light brown, about 3 minutes. Skim off any fat from the reduced stock, then add it to the pan and bring to a simmer. Cook gently, uncovered, for about 30 minutes. Whisk in the cream, return to a brisk simmer, and cook for 2 minutes. Remove from the heat. *At this point, the gravy can be kept warm in the top of a double boiler set over hot, but not boiling, water, until serving time, not longer than 30 minutes.*

Buttermilk Mashed Potatoes

preparation **30** minutes | cooking **25** minutes | **8–10** servings

Potatoes should be mashed just before serving, while the turkey is resting and the sauce is reheating. The last-minute attention yields a better consistency.

tools | vegetable peeler (optional) | chef's knife | kitchen shears | large saucepan | small saucepan | colander | potato masher | wooden spoon

2 kg (4 lb) potatoes, scrubbed, peeled if desired, and cut into 5-cm (2-in) chunks

Sea salt and ground white pepper

430 ml (14 fl oz) buttermilk

4 Tbsp (60 g /2 oz) unsalted butter, cut into 4 chunks

2 Tbsp finely snipped fresh chives

Put the potatoes in a large saucepan with cold water to cover by 2.5 cm (1 in) and 1 Tbsp salt. Bring to a boil over high heat. Cook until the potatoes are tender when pierced with the tip of a knife, 15–20 minutes.

Combine the buttermilk, butter, 1½ tsp salt, and ½ tsp white pepper in a small saucepan. Bring just to a boil and remove from the heat.

Drain the potatoes well. Return them to the pan and place over low heat. Let steam for 2–3 minutes, shaking the pan occasionally. Mash until smooth or still slightly chunky, according to taste. *At this point, the potatoes can be covered and held in a warm spot for up to 15 minutes.* When ready to serve, make sure the buttermilk mixture is hot, then stir it and the chives into the potatoes. Serve at once.

Braised Chard with Garlic

preparation **25** minutes | cooking **15** minutes | **8–10** servings

These earthy greens complement the sweet cranberry relish and creamy mashed potatoes. If you prefer to temper the bite of the garlic, add it to the chard ribs and onions halfway through the cooking time, instead of with the leaves.

tools | chef's knife | large sauté pan | wooden spatula | tongs

1 kg (2 lb) Swiss chard, tough stems removed

3 Tbsp olive oil

1 large onion, halved and thinly sliced

Salt and freshly ground pepper

10 cloves garlic, thinly sliced

Cut the ribs out of the chard leaves. Slice the ribs crosswise about 1 cm (⅜ in) thick. Stack the chard leaves and cut them crosswise into 12-mm (½-in) shreds. *At this point, the sliced chard can be refrigerated for up to 2 hours.*

Heat the olive oil in a large, heavy sauté pan over medium-low heat. Add the onion, chopped chard ribs, and 1 tsp salt. Cook for about 10 minutes, stirring occasionally, until tender-crisp. Add the chard leaves and the garlic, cover the pan, and cook for 5–6 minutes, turning over with tongs halfway through. The chard should be tender but not soggy. Turn again gently to mix, taste and adjust the seasoning, and serve at once.

Pecan Tart

preparation **1** hour | cooking **1** hour **10** minutes | **8–10** servings

Pecan pies can sometimes be tooth-achingly sweet, but this contemporary version tones down the sugar and plays up the flavour of the pecans. Of course, a dollop of bourbon-laced whipped cream would not go amiss as a garnish.

tools | chef's knife | small saucepan | 28-cm (11-in) tart pan | food processor | rolling pin | fork | pie weights (optional) | mixing bowl | whisk | baking sheet | wire rack

FOR THE CRUST

Vegetable oil spray

235 g (7½ oz) flour

2 Tbsp sugar

½ tsp salt

185 g (6 oz) cold unsalted butter, cut into 2-cm (¾-in) chunks

2–4 Tbsp ice water

FOR THE FILLING

440 g (14 oz) firmly packed dark brown sugar

3 large eggs plus 1 large egg yolk, lightly beaten

4 Tbsp (60 g /2 oz) unsalted butter, melted

1 Tbsp vanilla extract (essence)

⅛ tsp salt

290 g (9⅓ oz) pecan halves and pieces, lightly toasted

To make the crust, preheat the oven to 165°C (325°F). Lightly spray an 28-cm (11-in) tart pan with removable sides with oil.

In a food processor, combine the flour, sugar, and salt. Pulse briefly to blend. Add the cold butter pieces and pulse until the mixture resembles grated cheese. With the motor running, quickly drizzle the ice water through the feed tube 1 Tbsp at a time, using just enough to bring the dough together in a shaggy mass. (The crust may also be made in a stand mixer or by hand, using a pastry blender or 2 knives to cut in the butter.)

Turn the dough out onto a lightly floured board and roll out into a 30- to 33-cm (12- to 13-in) round, giving the round an occasional quarter-turn to prevent it from sticking to the work surface. Transfer the dough, without stretching, to the tart pan, fitting it into the corners and slightly over the edges of the pan. Fold in the excess dough and press firmly to reinforce the sides; prick the tart shell in several places with the tines of a fork. Line the pastry with foil or parchment (baking) paper and fill with pie weights or raw rice. Place on a foil-lined baking sheet and bake just until the edges of the dough lose their shine, 10–12 minutes; it should be only very lightly browned. Remove from the oven, remove the foil and weights, and set aside. *At this point, the tart shell can be wrapped and refrigerated for up to 2 days or frozen for up to 1 week. No need to thaw before filling and baking.* To bake at once, leave the oven set at 165°C (325°F).

To make the filling, in a bowl, whisk together the brown sugar, eggs, egg yolk, melted butter, vanilla, and salt until well blended. Stir in the pecans. Pour the filling into the tart shell and bake until the crust is golden and the filling is just set, about 1 hour. Let cool completely on a wire rack. *At this point, the tart can be refrigerated for up to 24 hours. Let the tart return to room temperature before serving.* Cut into wedges to serve.

bourbon whipped cream Using an electric mixer, beat 250 ml (8 fl oz) double cream until stiff peaks form when the beater is lifted, drizzling in 2 tsp best-quality bourbon during the last few seconds of the beating.

Celebration dinner

Celebrate any special occasion in memorable style with this satisfying feast, featuring a mouthwateringly tender beef tenderloin and a light, smooth frozen soufflé.

Smoked Trout Toast Points

Frisée Salad with Herbed Fresh Cheese

Beef Fillet with Mushroom Sauce

Roasted Carrots

Green Beans with Lemon Vinaigrette

Grand Marnier Frozen Soufflé

White-wine pairing: Viognier

Red-wine pairing: Cabernet Sauvignon or Bordeaux

SERVES 8

Savour each course of this meal with a carefully selected wine, served, if possible, in the glass that shows it off best, from slender champagne flutes to tall, generously proportioned Cabernet glasses.

Ahead of time

General party prep

Week of the party

- Assemble the necessary serving pieces:
  - *Platter for smoked trout toasts*
  - *Platter for roast beef*
  - *Sauceboat for sauce*
  - *Serving dish for carrots*
  - *Platter for green beans*
  - *Soufflé dish for frozen soufflé*
- Clean the house.

Food and drink

Week of the party

- Visit a wine merchant to select the bottles you need. With the toast points, plan to serve champagne or a classic aperitif such as Campari and orange juice. With the salad, offer a full-bodied white wine with strong character, such as a California Viognier. The beef deserves a serious red wine: perhaps a fine California Cabernet or a French Bordeaux.

Up to 3 days ahead

- Make a list and go grocery shopping.

Up to 1 day ahead

- Make herbed fresh cheese.
- Wash, spin dry, and chill frisée.
- Make frozen soufflé.

Day of the party	After the party starts
Early in the day ■ Arrange flowers, fruit, and candles around the house. ■ Set the table. Arrange wineglasses with the glass that will be used first on the far left; make sure the glasses are spotless. ■ Determine the seating order and make place cards. ■ Set up post-dinner coffee service. Place the coffee service and small plates on a table or sideboard near the dinner table, so that they are at hand after the dinner plates are cleared.	**After guests arrive** ■ One spouse serves appetizers and aperitifs in the living room area, while the other spouse finishes preparing the food. ■ When one host has plated the salad and placed it on the table, the other can usher guests to the table.
Up to 4 hours ahead ■ Make and refrigerate carrot butter. ■ Make cream cheese mixture for toast points. ■ Make mushroom sauce up to, but not including, the cream. **Up to 2 hours ahead** ■ Cut carrots and toss with flavouring. ■ Trim and precook green beans; make vinaigrette. ■ Make toast points. ■ Remove fillet, cream cheese mixture, and carrot butter from refrigerator. **Up to ½ hour ahead** ■ Chill white wine in ice water. ■ Put beef and carrots in oven. ■ Cut toast points. **Just before the party starts** ■ Assemble toast points and salad.	**After guests arrive** ■ Finish cooking beans. ■ Warm mushroom sauce and add cream. **After dinner** ■ To complete the menu, add a single-cheese course. Consider Camembert served with dried apricots, Manchego with black cherry jam, shards of Parmesan with honey, or Shropshire or Maytag blue with walnut bread. Offering a cheese with a wine or even a beer from the same region is an interesting way to find a natural pairing.

Smoked Trout Toast Points

preparation **25** minutes | cooking **7** minutes | **8** servings (20 bites)

This classic appetizer is deceptively simple to make. For the easiest possible version, use pumpernickel cocktail bread and don't toast it, as it doesn't take well to toasting. Just call them canapés instead of toast points. If you cut the bread ahead of time, keep it covered to prevent the edges from curling. For a more colourful presentation, substitute thinly sliced smoked salmon for the smoked trout.

tools | salad spinner | serrated bread knife | food processor | baking sheets

60 g (2 oz) loosely packed watercress sprigs, leaves and tender stems only, spun dry

60 g (2 oz) cream cheese, softened

60 g (2 oz) ricotta cheese

½ tsp sea salt

¼ tsp ground white pepper

5 slices wholemeal bread, crusts trimmed, quartered on the diagonal, or 10 slices cocktail-size pumpernickel bread, crusts trimmed, halved on the diagonal

315 g (10 oz) smoked trout, skinned and flaked with a fork into large chunks

Reserve 20 attractive sprigs of the watercress for garnish; place them on a damp paper towel, cover with cling film, and refrigerate until serving time. In a food processor, combine the remaining watercress with the cream cheese, ricotta, salt, and pepper. Pulse until smooth. *At this point, the cream cheese mixture can be refrigerated for up to 4 hours. Let sit at room temperature for 30 minutes before spreading.*

If using whole-wheat bread, preheat the oven to 165°C (325°F). Lay the bread on baking sheets and toast until only just beginning to turn golden, 5–7 minutes; don't overcook them, or they will shatter when you spread the cheese. The toasts can be covered with cling film (to prevent them from becoming brittle) and held at room temperature for up to 2 hours. If you are using cocktail pumpernickel slices, leave them untoasted.

Spread each piece of bread thickly with about 2 Tbsp of the watercress mixture, spreading it all the way to the edges, and place on a platter. Top each with a few pieces of smoked trout and a sprig of watercress. Serve within 10 minutes.

colour-coded glasses Tie short lengths of ribbon in complementary colours around the stems of champagne flutes or wineglasses, for a gift-wrapped look. Choose different colours for the white and red wineglasses, and for dessert wine goblets, if using. Or, choose different colours for different guests so they can keep track of their many glasses!

Frisée Salad with Herbed Fresh Cheese

preparation **30** minutes | **8** servings

Fresh and pretty, this salad is the perfect opener to the rich, meaty, and meltingly tender main course that will follow. For the crispest salad greens, rinse in very cool water, spin dry, and wrap in paper towels (this can be done up to one day ahead). Refrigerate until just before serving time and then gently tear into bite-sized pieces with your thumb and forefinger. Do not bunch the delicate greens between your fists and pull them apart, which would crush and bruise them.

tools | salad spinner | kitchen shears | chef's knife | medium mixing bowl | whisk | large mixing bowl | tongs | 2 spoons

8 small heads frisée

375 g (12 oz) *fromage blanc* or 345 g (11 oz) fresh goat cheese, softened

2 Tbsp milk

1 Tbsp finely snipped fresh chives

1 Tbsp finely chopped fresh parsley

1 tsp finely chopped fresh tarragon

1 small shallot, minced

1 Tbsp extra-virgin olive oil, plus 80 ml (3 fl oz)

2 Tbsp red wine vinegar

Salt and freshly ground pepper

Remove the outer leaves from each head of frisée until you reach the pale inner heart. Reserve the outer leaves for another use and tear the inner leaves into large bite-sized pieces; you should have about 240 g (4 oz).

In a medium bowl, combine the *fromage blanc* and milk and beat until smooth. Add the chives, parsley, tarragon, shallot, 1 Tbsp olive oil, 1½ tsp of the vinegar, ¼ tsp salt, and a little pepper. Whisk together until smooth. *At this point, the cheese mixture can be refrigerated for up to 1 day. Whisk again and let sit at room temperature for 10 minutes before using.*

In a large bowl, toss the frisée with the ⅓ cup olive oil and ½ tsp salt until coated. Sprinkle with the remaining 1½ Tbsp vinegar and pepper to taste. Toss again.

Using tongs, divide the salad among individual plates. Using 2 spoons, scoop up and place atop each salad 3 large dollops of the fresh cheese. Serve at once.

Beef Fillet with Mushroom Sauce

soaking **20** minutes | standing **1** hour | cooking **1** hour **25** minutes | **8** servings

Tender, mild beef fillet lends itself to a richly flavoured sauce. To save room in the oven, instructions are given for cooking the beef and carrots (page 158) together.

tools | small saucepan | chef's knife | coffee filter | small glass measuring jug | large saucepan | wooden spatula | kitchen string | roasting rack | rimmed baking sheet | brush | instant-read thermometer | large spatula | sauce whisk | carving set

30 g (1 oz) dried porcini mushrooms (ceps)

375 ml (12 fl oz) very hot water

750 g (1½ lb) cremini mushrooms, stems removed and caps brushed clean

2 Tbsp unsalted butter, plus 3 Tbsp melted

3 large shallots, minced

Sea salt and freshly ground pepper

125 ml (4 fl oz) brandy or Cognac

1 can (470 ml/15 fl oz) beef consommé

1 centre-cut beef tenderloin, about 1.75 kg (3½ lb)

1–2 tsp coarsely cracked peppercorns

250 ml (8 fl oz) double cream

1 tsp white or black truffle oil

Soak the porcini in the hot water for 20 minutes. Meanwhile, quarter the cremini caps (or, if they are on the large side, chop coarsely). Drain the porcini, pouring the soaking water through a coffee filter into a small glass measuring jug and reserving it. Squeeze excess water from the porcini and chop finely.

In a large saucepan, melt 2 Tbsp butter over medium heat. Add the shallots and sauté until softened, 4–5 minutes. Add both types of mushrooms, season with salt and pepper, and cook, stirring occasionally, until they release moisture, about 10 minutes. Add the brandy, raise the heat to high, and bring to a simmer. Stir for about 5 minutes, or until the liquid has almost completely evaporated. Add the porcini soaking water and the consommé; adjust the heat so the liquid simmers briskly and cook, uncovered, for about 30 minutes. *At this point, the sauce can be refrigerated for up to 4 hours. Rewarm before proceeding with the recipe.*

If the roast has a skinny end, fold it under and tie with string to create a fairly uniform diameter. Pat the roast dry and place it on a rack on a rimmed baking sheet. Brush all over with the 3 Tbsp melted butter and season generously with salt and cracked peppercorns, pressing gently to help the seasoning adhere. Let stand at room temperature for ½–1 hour. To cook the carrots (page 158) with the beef, scatter the carrots underneath and around the sides of the rack.

Preheat the oven to 230°C (450°F). When hot, roast the beef and carrots until a thermometer inserted into the thickest part of the roast reads 46°C (115°F) for rare, or 52°C (125°F) for medium-rare; start checking the temperature after 20 minutes. (If you cook the beef without the carrots, the roasting time will be slightly shorter.) Halfway through cooking, stir and turn the carrots over with a large spatula. Transfer the beef to a cutting board, tent with foil, and let rest for 10 minutes. If needed, roast the carrots for 5–10 minutes more, until golden.

While the beef is roasting and resting, finish the sauce. Whisk the cream into the sauce, season lightly with salt and pepper, and simmer over medium-low heat until slightly thickened, 10–15 minutes. Remove from the heat; taste and adjust the seasoning. Whisk in the truffle oil, cover, and set aside until serving time.

Cut beef into thick slices and transfer to a platter. Spoon some of the mushroom sauce over the sliced beef and/or pass the sauce in a sauceboat at the table.

Roasted Carrots

preparation **30** minutes | cooking **25** minutes | **8** side-dish servings

Roasting brings out a sweet, caramelised flavour in carrots that you may never have expected. The herb butter adds a savoury touch to the finished dish, but feel free to omit it for a simpler, earthier flavour. Do not use bagged "baby" carrots for this dish, which are large carrots that have been ground down to size. You want crisp, slender true young carrots, which are sweeter. If you like, trim the carrots and toss them with the salt, pepper, and thyme up to 2 hours before roasting—the flavour will benefit from the additional time.

tools | chef's knife | kitchen shears | mixing bowls | large roasting pan

4 Tbsp (60 g/2 oz) unsalted butter, softened

1 large shallot, finely chopped

2 Tbsp finely snipped fresh chives

1½ tsp finely chopped fresh rosemary

1 clove garlic, minced

2 kg (4 lb) slender young carrots, scrubbed

60 ml (2 fl oz) extra-virgin olive oil

2 tsp sea salt

1 tsp freshly ground pepper

3 large sprigs fresh thyme

In a small bowl, combine the butter, shallot, chives, rosemary, and garlic. Mash together well. *At this point, the butter mixture can be refrigerated for up to 4 hours.*

Trim the carrots and cut into matchsticks: Cut the carrots crosswise into 5-cm (2-in) lengths, then cut lengthwise to yield sticks 6 mm (¼ in) wide and thick. Place in a large bowl. Add the olive oil and toss to coat. Add the salt, pepper, and thyme sprigs and toss again. *At this point, the carrots can be held for up to 2 hours.*

Preheat the oven to 200°C (400°F). Transfer the carrots to a large roasting pan, preferably metal or enameled cast iron. To roast the carrots alongside the beef fillet (page 156), scatter the carrots underneath and around the sides of the rack holding the beef. Roast, turning the mass of carrots over once halfway through the cooking time with a wide spatula, until nicely browned, 20–25 minutes.

Transfer the carrots to a serving dish, add the herbed butter, and toss to coat the carrots with the butter. Serve at once.

Green Beans with Lemon Vinaigrette

preparation **30** minutes | standing **5** minutes | cooking **14** minutes | **8** side-dish servings

Here, a tart and citrusy lemon vinaigrette elevates simple green beans. If you cannot find slender haricot verts, substitute standard green beans and cut them into 5-cm (2-in) lengths on the diagonal, or run them through a bean slicer, a small tool that makes slicing these stocky beans an easy chore.

tools | chef's knife | citrus reamer | box grater | serrated utility knife | large pot | large bowl | colander | baking sheet | mixing bowl | whisk | large frying pan | wooden spatula

1.25 kg (2½ lb) haricot verts or other slender green beans, stem ends trimmed

1½ Tbsp fresh lemon juice

Salt and freshly ground pepper

80 ml (3 fl oz) extra-virgin olive oil

1 tsp finely grated or minced lemon zest

2 Tbsp unsalted butter

1 shallot, finely chopped

2 plum tomatoes, cored, seeded, and cut into small pieces

Bring a large pot of lightly salted water to the boil. Have ready a bowl of ice water. Plunge the beans into the boiling water and cook for 4 minutes. Drain beans in a colander and immediately transfer to the ice water to stop the cooking. Let stand for 5 minutes, then drain again and spread the beans on a paper towel–lined baking sheet. *At this point, the beans can be refrigerated for up to 2 hours. Remove from the refrigerator just before serving time.*

In a bowl, whisk together the lemon juice, ¼ tsp salt, and ¼ tsp pepper. Slowly drizzle in the olive oil, whisking constantly until emulsified. Stir in the lemon zest. *At this point, the vinaigrette can be held at room temperature for up to 1 hour, or for up to 2 hours in the refrigerator. Whisk again before proceeding.*

About 10 minutes before serving time, melt the butter in a large frying pan over medium heat. Add the shallot and tomatoes and cook, stirring occasionally, until slightly softened, about 3 minutes. Add the blanched beans and cook, stirring occasionally, just until heated through and glazed.

Transfer the green beans to a serving platter and drizzle with the lemon vinaigrette. Toss together gently and serve.

Grand Marnier Frozen Soufflé

preparation **1** hour | chilling **12** hours | **8** servings

If an oven-risen soufflé is the ultimate last-minute dessert, a frozen soufflé is its ultimate make-ahead counterpart. In fact, you'll need to make this several hours before serving to give it time to chill properly. Using a collar allows you to fill the dish above the rim, so the whipped mixture mimics the puffed top of a traditional baked soufflé.

tools | box grater | chef's knife | large soufflé dish | parchment (baking) paper | tape | mixing bowls | whisk | medium saucepan | balloon whisk | rubber spatula

Vegetable oil spray

8 large egg yolks

185 g (6 oz) sugar

Finely grated zest of 2 large oranges, preferably organic, scrubbed

180 ml (6 fl oz) Grand Marnier or another orange-flavoured liqueur

500 ml (16 fl oz) double cream

5 large egg whites (see Note)

Ice cubes as needed

75 g (2½ oz) finely chopped toasted almonds (page 122)

Sliced kumquats and toasted sliced (flaked) almonds for garnish (optional)

Fit a 1.5 litre (48–fl oz/1½-qt) soufflé dish with a collar. Cut strips of baking parchment or waxed paper about 5 cm (2 in) longer than the circumference of the soufflé dish. Fold the strip in half lengthwise and seal the open edge by folding it over, forming a 2.5 cm (1 in) flap. Tape or tie the paper around the soufflé dish so it rises 5 cm (2 in) above the rim. Spray the inside of the soufflé dish with oil and sprinkle with sugar, knocking out any excess.

Fill a large bowl halfway with ice cubes and cold water. In a large non-aluminium bowl, whisk together the egg yolks, half of the sugar, and the orange zest. Whisk in the Grand Marnier and place the bowl over, but not touching, barely simmering water in a saucepan. Cook, whisking constantly, until the mixture is pale and thick enough to coat the back of a spoon, 7–10 minutes. Remove the bowl from the heat and nest it in the ice-water bath. Gently whisk the mixture frequently, scraping down the sides of the bowl as needed, until it begins to thicken, 6–8 minutes.

Meanwhile, using a balloon whisk or an electric mixer on medium-high speed, lightly whip the cream in a large chilled bowl until soft peaks form when the whisk is lifted. Set aside. In a separate, large, spotlessly clean bowl, using a clean balloon whisk or the clean beaters of a mixer on medium-high speed, beat the egg whites until light and foamy. Continue beating, gradually adding the remaining sugar, until stiff, glossy peaks form when the whisk is lifted.

Carefully fold about one-third each of the whipped cream and egg whites into the cooled egg yolk mixture to lighten it. Then fold in the remaining whipped cream and egg whites just until combined. Scoop the mixture into the prepared soufflé dish and smooth the top out to the edge of the collar. The mixture should come about halfway up the inside of the collar. Freeze until firm, about 4 hours or up to overnight. Drape the top of the collar with cling film if freezing overnight.

When ready to serve, carefully remove the collar. Gently press the chopped almonds into the exposed sides of the soufflé. Garnish the top with kumquats and sliced almonds, if desired. Scoop with a large spoon onto individual dessert plates.

Note: Frozen soufflés are made with raw egg whites. See warning on page 184.

GINGER
CHAMPAGNE COCKTAIL
POUR 2 TSP GINGER LIQUEUR
INTO A FLUTE, ADD A STRIP
OF LEMON PEEL AND TOP
UP WITH COLD CHAMPAGNE
CHEERS!

New Year's Eve party

New Year's Eve is the time to pull out all the stops and host a truly elegant party: the party that all your friends will remember and reminisce about for years to come.

Champagne Cocktail Bar

Tenderloin Canapés with Rémoulade

Blini with Caviar and Sour Cream

Chocolate-Dipped Coconut Macaroons

SERVES 6–8

Plan this cocktail party as either a pre-dinner or post-dinner New Year's Eve gathering, depending on the celebratory habits of your circle of friends and family.

Ahead of time

General party prep

Week of the party

- Assemble the necessary serving pieces:
  - *At least 6–8 champagne flutes*
  - *Platters for oysters, blini, canapés, and cheese course*
  - *Large plate or platter for macaroons*
- Select music for the party. Play jazz classics: George Gershwin, early Louis Armstrong, and Ella Fitzgerald singing Cole Porter tunes.
- Plan decorations and clean the house.
- Assemble bar: ice buckets, trays, printed recipes, small plates for garnishes.

Food and drink

Up to 1 month ahead

- Make ginger vodka, if desired.

Up to 2 weeks ahead

- Make raspberry vodka, if desired.

Week of the party

- Stock up on champagne and other beverages.
- Caviar choices are not as simple as they used to be. With plenty of time before the party, research the domestic and international choices available. Visit a responsible purveyor and ask for advice, then set a budget to prevent the party from breaking the bank.

Up to 3 days ahead

- Make a list and go grocery shopping.
- Make macaroons. Store between sheets of baking parchment in an airtight container in the fridge.
- Chill champagne flutes.
- Make *rémoulade* sauce and cocktail sauce.

Day of the party

Early in the day

- Set up coffee service.
- Play a round of "rock, paper, scissors" to determine who makes the ice run.

Up to 1 hour ahead

- Fill waterproof backup champagne container (or bathtub) with ice and place bottles in ice.

Up to 2 hours ahead

- Make batter for blini.
- Toast canapé bases (and don't let them get too brown).

Up to 1 hour ahead

- Season beef and let stand at room temperature.
- Place champagne in ice water, cover with towels, and twirl bottles occasionally.
- Place vodkas and/or liqueurs and garnishes on bar.

Up to ½ hour ahead

- Roast tenderloin, let rest, and slice.
- Cook blini.

Just before the party starts

- Assemble tenderloin canapés.
- Assemble blini and caviar platter.

After the party starts

After guests arrive

- Place a platter of tenderloin canapés on a central table.

During the party

- Pass by the champagne bar regularly to top up ice buckets, check supplies, and clear bottle-opening debris.

As guests arrive

- Remove macaroons from refrigerator to come to room temperature.
- To start the party off, serve fresh oysters with the champagne cocktails. Arrange oysters on the half shell on a bed of ice and offer cocktail sauce, or make oyster shooters: put small oysters (such as Kumamotos) into shot glasses with a healthy amount of cocktail sauce and a squeeze of fresh lime, then top with caviar or dill.
- To complete the menu and ensure that your guests have plenty to eat along with their cocktails, serve a classic French cheese plate. Offer 3 styles of cheeses made with 3 different types of milk: perhaps a soft, fresh goat cheese with fresh or dried figs, a semi-soft cow's milk cheese such as Port-Salut with blueberries, and a Petit Basque sheep's milk cheese with quince paste. Thinly slice a baguette or two.

Champagne Cocktail Bar

preparation **20** minutes | infusing **2** weeks–**1** month (optional) | **6–8** servings

For champagne cocktails, feel free to use any type of good-quality sparkling wine—from Spanish cava *or Italian Prosecco to Californian sparkling wine.*

tools | vegetable peeler | chef's knife | strainer | ice buckets | channel knife

2 or 3 bottles (750 ml/ 24 fl oz) each) very cold sparkling wine

1 bottle (750 ml/ 24 fl oz) best-quality cognac

Raspberry vodka (below) or Chambord

Ginger vodka (below) or ginger liqueur

GARNISHES

Raspberries

Lemon twists (page 41)

Turbinado or Demerara sugar cubes

If there is room in the refrigerator or freezer, chill 8 champagne flutes for about an hour, or longer if desired. Put the sparkling wine, cognac, raspberry vodka, and ginger vodka bottles into ice buckets filled with half water and half ice. Place the raspberries and lemon twists on small platters lined with folded, damp napkins, and the sugar cubes in a small bowl.

Guests can choose to make one of the three following cocktails. Write out the instructions on cards to display at the bar:

For a Raspberry Champagne Cocktail: Place 2 tsp raspberry vodka in a flute. Drop in a raspberry and top up with cold sparkling wine.

For a Classic Champagne Cocktail: Place a sugar cube in a flute and drizzle it with 1–2 tsp of Cognac. Top up with cold sparkling wine.

For a Ginger Champagne Cocktail: Place 2 tsp ginger vodka in a flute, add a lemon twist, and top up with cold sparkling wine.

raspberry and ginger vodkas To make your own raspberry vodka, drop 250 g (8 oz) fresh raspberries into ½ bottle (375 ml) premium vodka. Let stand at room temperature for 2 weeks, then place in the freezer the night before you plan to serve the cocktails. Similarly, to make ginger vodka, place 4 thick slices (about 6 mm / ¼ in thick) peeled fresh ginger into ½ bottle premium vodka and let stand at room temperature for 1 month. Strain into a clean bottle and place in the freezer the night before the party.

Tenderloin Canapés with Rémoulade

preparation **30** minutes | cooking **22** minutes | resting **5** minutes | **6–8** servings (16 bites)

Although rémoulade was invented in France, it has been adopted widely by other cuisines. The New Orleans version uses Creole mustard, cayenne, and paprika for spiciness and red colour, and the Danes love to eat it with beef, as is done here. For a more Scandinavian version, try making these canapés with rye bread.

tools | bread knife | chef's knife | brush | baking sheet | roasting rack | roasting pan | small bowl | whisk

500 g (1 lb) sirloin steak

2 Tbsp extra-virgin olive oil

Salt and freshly ground pepper

16 slices baguette, 12 mm (½ in) thick (about 1 baguette)

125 ml (4 fl oz) mayonnaise

2 tsp finely chopped spring onion, dark green part only

1 pickled gherkin, trimmed and finely chopped

1 tsp finely chopped fresh parsley

½ tsp Dijon mustard

¼ tsp prepared horseradish

¼ tsp Worcestershire sauce

Preheat the oven to 180°C (350°F). Pat the steak dry with paper towels. Brush on both sides with 1 Tbsp of the olive oil; season generously with salt and pepper. Let stand at room temperature for up to 1 hour while you prepare the bread.

Arrange the baguette slices on a baking sheet and brush lightly with the remaining 1 Tbsp olive oil. Season with salt and pepper. Bake until slightly softened but not golden, about 8 minutes. Transfer the canapés to a serving platter.

Preheat the grill and position the rack about 15 cm (6 in) from the heat source. Place the steak on a rack in a roasting pan. When the grill is very hot, grill the steak, turning once, until firm but still quite pink in the centre, about 7 minutes on each side. Transfer to a cutting board and let rest for 5 minutes, then slice *with* the grain into halves or thirds lengthwise, so each piece is about 5cm (2 in) wide. Turn the pieces and slice very thinly *across* the grain.

In a small bowl, whisk together the mayonnaise, spring onion, gherkin, parsley, mustard, horseradish, Worcestershire sauce, ⅛ tsp salt, and a tiny pinch of pepper. *At this point, the sauce can be covered tightly and refrigerated for up to 3 days.*

Curl or layer 2 or 3 slices of the steak on each canapé. Top each with a dollop of the *rémoulade* sauce and serve.

Blini with Caviar and Sour Cream

preparation **30** minutes | rising **1½** hours| cooking **5** minutes per batch | **6–8** servings

Originally a staple of high society in pre-Soviet Russia, blini were eagerly adopted by the wider international public generations ago, and their role as the classic vehicle for caviar has never been challenged. Because of recent restrictions on the Caspian Sea sturgeon harvest, iconic beluga, osetra, and sevruga caviar are now either rarely available or of uneven quality. Happily, farmed caviar from Europe and America is so good you may not miss the traditional Caspian varieties.

tools | small saucepan | instant-read thermometer (optional) | medium mixing bowl | kitchen towel | mixing bowl | balloon whisk | rubber spatula | large nonstick frying pan | small ladle

1 tsp quick-rise active dry yeast

125 ml (4 fl oz) warmed whole milk (40°–46°C /105°–115°F)

75 g (2½ oz) flour

¼ tsp salt

1 large egg, separated

2 Tbsp unsalted butter

125 g (4 oz) sour cream

125 g (4 oz) domestic or imported caviar

In a medium mixing bowl, combine the yeast, warm milk, flour, salt, and egg yolk. Stir together to blend and then whisk until smooth. Cover the bowl with a clean kitchen towel and let the batter rise in a warm place until it has doubled in bulk, about 1½ hours.

In a perfectly clean bowl, beat the egg white with a balloon whisk until stiff, pointed peaks form when the whisk is lifted. Using a rubber spatula, fold into the batter gently but thoroughly.

Melt about 2 tsp of the butter in a large nonstick frying pan over medium-low heat. (Alternatively, use a nonstick griddle, brushing lightly with melted butter.) Ladle 1 rounded Tbsp of the fluffy batter into the pan for each blini, being careful not to crowd the pan. Cook until the bottoms are lightly browned and bubbles have formed on the top, about 3 minutes. Flip the blini over and cook until browned on the second side, about 2 minutes longer. Transfer to a platter, cover with aluminium foil, and place in a low (95°C/200°F) oven to keep warm. Cook the remaining blini in the same way, adding butter to the pan as needed. You should have 18–20 small blini. *At this point, the blini can remain in the warm oven for up to 30 minutes before topping and serving.*

To serve, spread about 1 tsp sour cream over the top of each blini. Top each with a generous ½ tsp caviar. Arrange on a platter and serve at once.

caviar styles Basic black is always appropriate, but you can also use different flavours and colours of caviar: choose from—or mix and match—grey truffle caviar, green wasabi caviar, crimson beet caviar, golden north American whitefish roe, and the larger orange-red salmon roe. Echo the colours in the platters and cocktail napkins you use.

Chocolate-Dipped Coconut Macaroons

preparation **30** minutes | chilling **1½** hours | cooking **50** minutes | **6–8** servings (12 cookies)

These old-fashioned cookies are the perfect make-ahead morsels to accompany post-midnight toasting. They also partner well with a cup of expertly brewed espresso, for the New Year's journey home.

tools | chef's knife | 2 large baking sheets | parchment (baking) paper | mixing bowl | wooden spoon | silicone baking mat (optional) | wire rack | double boiler

375 g (12 oz) sweetened shredded dried coconut

185 g (6 oz) sugar

5 large egg whites, lightly beaten

1½ tsp vanilla extract (essence)

¼ tsp almond extract (essence)

250 g (8 oz) best-quality plain chocolate, finely chopped

Line a large rimmed baking sheet with parchment (baking) paper.

Combine the coconut, sugar, egg whites, and vanilla and almond extracts and mix well. Spread on the baking sheet and refrigerate until cold, about 30 minutes.

Preheat the oven to 150°C (300°F). Line another baking sheet with parchment paper or use a silicone baking mat. Using a 60-ml (2-fl oz) measuring cup, scoop and pack the coconut mixture into 12 small, rounded domes, and place them on the baking sheet. Bake until golden, about 30 minutes.

Transfer the cookies to a wire rack and let cool completely. Line the pan with a fresh sheet of parchment (baking) paper.

Put the chocolate in the top of a double boiler placed over (but not touching) barely simmering water. Stir until melted and smooth, then remove from the heat. Dip the bottom of each macaroon in the melted chocolate to a depth of 6 mm (¼ in). Place on the freshly lined pan, chocolate side down. Chill until the chocolate is firm, about 1 hour. *At this point, the macaroons can be held for up to 3 days. Cover and keep refrigerated; let stand at room temperature for 1 hour before serving.*

Patrick

Festive brunch

This menu, suitable for celebrating new engagements or old friends visiting from afar, is light on last-minute labour, leaving you plenty of time to spend with guests.

Blood Orange Mimosas

Bellinis

Buttermilk and Chive Biscuits

Red Pepper and Goat Cheese Frittata

Ham with Fig-Balsamic Glaze

SERVES 10–12

In Italy, the esteemed Bellini is always made with Italy's sparkling white wine, Prosecco, and this would make a fine choice for both of the morning cocktails on this menu.

Ahead of time

General party prep

Week of the party

- Assemble the necessary serving pieces:

  At least 10–12 champagne flutes

  Platters for frittata and ham

  Basket or platter for biscuits

- Select music for the party. Try Baroque chamber music, such as Bach's Brandenburg concertos.
- Clean the house and plan decorations and favours.

Up to 1 day ahead

- Assemble containers and glassware for serving mimosas and Bellinis.

Food and drink

Week of the party

- Stock up on sparkling wine and other beverages. When mixing mimosas or Bellinis, the delicately nuanced flavours of a true French Champagne from the region of the same name would be obscured by the fruit juice(s), so select a sparkling wine from Spain, Italy, Australia, or California.

Up to 3 days ahead

- Make a list and go grocery shopping.

Up to 1 day ahead

- Cook pasta for frittata; toss with oil.
- Make frittata; let cool, cover, and refrigerate.

	Day of the party	After the party starts
	Early in the day ■ Place a bar at the opposite end of the room from the buffet, to encourage the flow of guests. ■ Roll up cutlery place settings inside napkins and tie. ■ Set up service for coffee and tea service to offer throughout the brunch. ■ Make a run for ice. **Up to 1 hour ahead** ■ Fill a large galvanized bucket (or your bathtub) with ice to hold backup bottles of champagne.	**During the party** ■ Circulate often to pick up used plates and glasses, keeping the party space tidy and attractive.
	Up to 3 hours ahead ■ Squeeze orange juice and refrigerate. ■ Bring ham to room temperature. **Up to 2 hours ahead** ■ Bake ham and hold before finishing. **Up to 1 hour ahead** ■ Place sparkling wine in ice water. ■ Bring frittata to room temperature or warm in a low oven, if desired. **Up to ½ hour ahead** ■ Glaze and finish baking ham. **Just before the party starts** ■ Make biscuits.	**As guests arrive** ■ Stir orange juice to recombine. ■ Cut first 10 or 15 slices of ham. ■ Offer water steeped with mint sprigs or cucumber slices.

Blood Orange Mimosas

preparation **15** minutes | **10–12** servings

The mimosa is the perfect cocktail for putting on the Ritz—that's where this concoction was invented. When blood oranges are out of season, choose juicy Valencia oranges.

tools | citrus reamer | fine-mesh sieve | jug | champagne flutes

625 ml (20 fl oz) fresh blood orange juice (6–8 oranges), well chilled

2 bottles (750 ml /24 fl oz each) sparkling wine such as *cava*, Prosecco, or California sparkling wine, chilled

Tiny fresh mint sprigs for garnish

If desired, squeeze the oranges up to 3 hours ahead of time and refrigerate.

If the orange juice has a lot of pulp in it, or you prefer a very clean look in the glass, strain the blood orange juice through a fine-mesh sieve. Put into an attractive jug and nestle securely in a large container of crushed ice on the table or buffet. Place 1 bottle of sparkling wine on either side and provide champagne flutes for guests to pour their own mimosas. Place the mint sprigs on a small plate lined with a cold, damp cloth napkin.

Bellinis

preparation **10** minutes | cooking **5** minutes | **10–12** servings

The Bellini has a more certain pedigree than most cocktails: it was created in 1948 by Harry Cipriani at Harry's Bar in Venice. There is no more enjoyable way to start the day!

tools | chef's knife | citrus reamer | blender | jug | champagne flutes

3 ripe white peaches, stoned but not peeled, cut into 2.5-cm (1-in) cubes

1 Tbsp fresh lemon juice

1 Tbsp simple syrup (below)

2 bottles (750 ml /24 fl oz each) sparkling wine such as *cava*, Prosecco, or California sparkling wine, chilled

Place the peaches, lemon juice, and simple syrup in a blender and process until smooth. Pour into a jug and nestle securely in a large container of crushed ice on the table or buffet. Place 1 bottle of sparkling wine on either side and provide champagne flutes for guests to pour their own beverages. Instruct guests to fill a glass about one-third full with peach purée, then top off with sparkling wine and stir gently to combine.

simple syrup A standard behind every bar, simple syrup provides a sweet flavour to offset the strong and the sour ones that make up many of the world's greatest cocktails. To make simple syrup, combine equal parts sugar and water in a saucepan and place over low heat. Stir until the sugar is completely dissolved. Remove from the heat and let cool to room temperature. Pour into a clean jar or other airtight container. Sugar syrup will keep, tightly capped, in the refrigerator for up to 2 months.

Buttermilk and Chive Biscuits

preparation **20** minutes | cooking **14** minutes | **10–12** servings (20 biscuits)

For a heavenly accompaniment to their citrus cocktails, suggest that guests break apart one of these savoury biscuits, slather it with golden-yellow butter, and layer it with slivers of thinly sliced, salty-sweet ham.

tools | chef's knife | small saucepan | kitchen shears | fine-mesh sieve | mixing bowl | pastry blender | dough scraper | baking sheet | brush

Preheat the oven to 230°C (450°F). Sift together the flour, baking powder, baking soda, and salt into a bowl. Add the cold butter and, using a pastry blender or 2 knives, cut it into the flour until the mixture resembles coarse meal. Add the chives and toss to distribute, then stir in the buttermilk just until the dry ingredients are moistened.

Lightly flour your hands, gather the dough into a ball, and transfer to a lightly floured work surface. Using your hands, form the dough into a rectangle about 12 mm (½ in) thick and roughly 28 by 23 cm (11 by 9 in) in area. Using a dough scraper or a knife, cut the dough into 20 equal-sized pieces. Transfer to an ungreased baking sheet, leaving a little room in between the biscuits.

Brush the tops with the melted butter and bake until pale golden and puffed, about 14 minutes. Serve warm.

625 g (20 oz) flour

4 tsp baking powder

1 tsp baking soda (bicarbonate of soda)

1 tsp salt

185 g (6 oz) cold unsalted butter, diced, plus 2 Tbsp, melted

20 g (¾ oz) finely snipped fresh chives

375 ml (12 fl oz) plus 2 Tbsp buttermilk

butter for biscuits Using a vegetable peeler, shave curls of good butter and place on a small platter near the biscuits. Or, whip softened butter with a little maple syrup, spoon into a ramekin, and place alongside the biscuits.

Red Pepper and Goat Cheese Frittata

preparation **1** hour | cooking **1** hour **25** minutes | cooling **20** minutes | **10–12** servings

This hearty, rustic, yet impressive centrepiece dish makes a welcome addition to any morning get-together. Happily, it can be made well in advance. The frittata is especially delicious if made with fresh eggs from the farmers' market.

tools | chef's knife | box grater | large pot | colander | 25-cm (10-in) nonstick springform pan | large frying pan | mixing bowl | whisk | wire rack | small, thin-bladed knife (optional)

2 large red peppers (capsicums), seeded and quartered

60 g (2 oz) fine dried bread crumbs

2 Tbsp olive oil

500 g (1 lb) small firm courgettes, ends trimmed, coarsely grated

4 large cloves garlic, finely chopped

250 g (8 oz) soft, mild goat cheese, well chilled

105 g (3½ oz) ditalini, tubetti, or macaroni, cooked until just al dente, drained, and tossed with 2 tsp olive oil

10 g (⅓ oz) fresh basil chiffonade (page 101)

16 large eggs

250 g (8 oz) whole-milk ricotta cheese

1½ tsp fine sea salt

¾ tsp freshly ground pepper

2 Tbsp Dijon mustard

Trim away any obvious white ribs from the pepper quarters and dice 1½ of the peppers. Cut the remaining ½ pepper into narrow strips about 2.5 cm (1 in) long to use as a garnish.

Preheat the oven to 180°C (350°F). Generously oil a 25-cm (10-in) nonstick springform pan and coat it evenly with the bread crumbs, knocking out the excess.

Place a large frying pan over medium-high heat and add the olive oil. When it is very hot, add the diced pepper and the courgette and sauté just until the vegetables have released their moisture and it has evaporated but they are still brightly coloured, 2–3 minutes. Add the garlic and cook just until it releases its aroma, about 30 seconds. Remove from the heat.

Crumble the goat cheese or cut it into small pieces. In a bowl, combine the cooked ditalini, the goat cheese, and the basil. Toss to mix. Spoon the courgette mixture into the prepared pan, smoothing it gently, and spoon the goat cheese mixture in an even layer over the top.

In a bowl, whisk together the eggs, ricotta, salt and pepper, and mustard until smooth. Pour the egg mixture into the pan, taking care not to disturb the layers. Tap the pan gently to dislodge any air bubbles. Cover with foil and bake for 30 minutes, then remove the foil and bake for 20 minutes longer. Scatter the pepper julienne over the top and continue baking the frittata until it is a light golden brown and just firm in the centre, about 20 minutes longer. Let cool on a wire rack for 20 minutes, then loosen the sides with a small, thin-bladed knife, if necessary, and remove the springform ring. *At this point, you can let the frittata cool, cover it, and refrigerate it for up to overnight. For the best flavour, let it return to room temperature (or warm it in a low 95°C/200°F oven) before serving.* Slide the frittata onto a platter and cut into wedges. Serve warm or at room temperature.

Ham with Fig-Balsamic Glaze

preparation **15** minutes | cooking **1½** hours | **10–12** servings

A common feature of the generous breakfast spreads of the American South, a spiral-cut ham will have most guests revisiting a buffet at least once, if not more. Here, the balsamic glaze adds a deep, tart note to the salty-sweet meat.

tools | shallow roasting pan | small saucepan | wooden spoon | brush

1 fully cooked bone-in ham, 3.5–4 kg (7–8 lb), spiral sliced but preferably unglazed

250 ml (8 fl oz) fig balsamic vinegar (see below)

160 ml (5 fl oz) honey

Preheat the oven to 120°C (250°F). Place the ham in a shallow roasting pan and cover tightly with foil. Bake until heated through, about 22 minutes per kilo. *At this point, you can hold the ham at room temperature for up to 1 hour.*

In a small saucepan, combine the vinegar and honey and warm gently, stirring, until smooth and blended.

Remove the foil and brush the vinegar mixture all over the ham, working some of it in between the slices. Raise the oven temperature to 180°C (350°F) and heat, basting every 5 minutes, until the surface of the ham is dark and crusty, 10–15 minutes longer. Serve hot or warm.

fig balsamic glaze If prepared fig balsamic vinegar is unavailable, warm 220 g (7 oz) fig jam until liquid, then remove any fig chunks and reserve for another use (over ice cream is a delicious option). Stir in 80 ml (3 fl oz) balsamic vinegar and substitute for the glaze in the recipe above.

Glossary

Albariño: The Albariño (al-bar-*een*-yo) grape, usually grown in Portugal and in Galicia, Spain, makes a dry white wine that often has the aroma of almonds, apricots, or peaches. Its bracing acidity makes it a good match for some seafood and salads.

Ale: Compared to lager, the other main type of beer, ale tends to have a darker colour, a heavier body, and a higher alcohol content. Usually sold in brown or dark green tinted bottles to protect them from the effects of light, aromatic Belgian ales range from golden to a deep amber colour. Many are still made in small quantities in monasteries.

Angostura bitters: Made in Trinidad, this is the best known of several types of bitters, mixtures of herbs, spices, and other aromatic ingredients blended into an alcohol base. Intensely flavoured and very bitter, they are typically used to flavour cocktails.

Bandol rosé: Made from red wine grapes of several different varieties, often including Mourvèdre, Grenache, and Cinsault, this pink-tinged wine comes from the Bandol region of Provence in France. Fresh, fruity, and typically dry, it is traditionally served lightly chilled. If you can't find Bandol rosé, widely considered some of France's best, another French rosé can be substituted.

Beaujolais: Although any wine made in France's Beaujolais region, south of Burgundy, can be called a Beaujolais, the term most often refers to the fresh, fruity, light-bodied red wine, usually made from the Gamay grape, for which the region is famous.

Bordeaux: Any wine produced in Bordeaux, France's most famous winemaking region, is called a Bordeaux. The most famous are intensely flavoured reds made from a blend of Cabernet Sauvignon, Merlot, Petit Verdot, Cabernet Franc, and Malbec. These prized, and often expensive, reds are typically served with hearty meat dishes. White Bordeaux, on the other hand, are usually made from Sémillon and sauvignon blanc grapes.

Burgundy: Burgundy, which refers to any of the wines from France's Burgundy region, may be red or white. The best reds, with a rich, earthy perfume, tend to be made from Pinot Noir grapes. Burgundy whites are most often made from Chardonnay or sometimes Aligoté.

Cabernet Sauvignon: A robust red wine often described as fruity, spicy, or herbaceous, made from the same grape as the wines of Médoc and Graves in the Bordeaux region of France. Good with hearty red meat dishes, whether roasted, grilled, stewed, or braised.

Caper berries: Olive shaped and with long stems, caper berries are the fruit of the Mediterranean shrub that produces capers. They are sold pickled or salted and must be rinsed before using.

Casserole: These large, heavy round or oval pots with tight-fitting lids and two loop handles are used for slow cooking in the oven. Most are ceramic. When made of cast iron, they are generally called Dutch ovens or stew pots.

Channel knife: A small knife with a notched metal blade, a channel knife is useful for cutting long twists of peel from citrus fruits as well as carving fruits and vegetables for garnishes. Many citrus zesters have a notch on the side that can be used for the same purpose. If you don't have either, a vegetable peeler can be used instead.

Chardonnay: This rich and fruity white wine is made from the grape of the same name. Although some Chardonnays can be bracingly dry and flinty, others undergo a process called malolactic fermentation during the winemaking process, which can result in an oaky, buttery flavour and a rich mouth feel.

Cheesecloth (muslin): This gauzy fabric, available at most supermarkets and kitchenware stores, is usually used to strain food. Before using it, rinse it first in hot then in cool water, to remove any loose fibres and to keep it from absorbing too much liquid from the food being strained.

Cocktail shaker: This utensil for combining cocktail ingredients and chilling them is usually made out of glass, metal, or a combination of the two. A cobbler shaker consists of a tumbler, a fitted lid, and a strainer built into the lid. A Boston shaker, which most bartenders use, consists of a pint glass and a metal tumbler that fits on top of the glass. If you're using a Boston shaker, you'll need to use a strainer to remove the ice as you pour the drink.

Consommé: This clear, richly flavoured broth is made from beef, veal, poultry, or, rarely, fish stock. Since the process of clarifying the stock to make consommé can be time-consuming, many chefs choose to purchase prepared consommé, available in cartons along with other soups in most supermarkets.

Crabmeat: Cooked fresh crabmeat may be purchased from a good fish purveyor. Lump crabmeat consists of large, snowy white pieces from the crab's back legs. Backfin crabmeat, which comes from the crab's body and legs, comes in somewhat smaller pieces. Flake crabmeat, the least expensive type, is a mixture of white and somewhat darker meat in smaller pieces. Before using crabmeat, check it carefully for cartilage and shell fragments and gently squeeze it to remove excess moisture.

Dough scraper: Also known as a bench scraper, this tool has a rectangular steel blade about 15cm (6 in) wide, capped with a handle. The blade has a dull edge but is thin enough to cut through dough and other soft ingredients. It's often used to lift and turn dough as you knead it, and also makes short work of cleaning off a work surface.

Eggs, raw: Some preparations, such as the frozen soufflé in this book, call for uncooked eggs. In rare cases, raw eggs can be infected with salmonella bacteria, which can cause food poisoning. The risk is highest for the elderly, pregnant women, babies and young children, and anyone with a compromised immune system. Point this out to your guests and let them decide whether or not they would like to sample the dish.

Fennel: Also known as sweet fennel or finocchio, a fennel plant's leaves, seeds, and stems have a sweet, faint aniselike flavour. Similar in appearance and texture to celery, fennel has stems that overlap at the base to form a somewhat flat bulb with white to pale green ribbed layers. The leaves are light and feathery. It is available year-round but is at its peak from October to March. Select creamy-coloured bulbs topped by fresh-looking stems and feathery green tops.

Fromage blanc: Literally "white cheese," this French term refers to a wide variety of unripened creamy cheeses made from skim or whole milk, with or without cream added. Fromage blanc is commonly eaten flavoured with sugar as a simple dessert and is also used in cooking.

Garlic press: This hinged tool, which makes quick work of mincing peeled garlic cloves, consists of a perforated hopper and a plunger that squeezes the garlic through small holes. Choose a press that feels comfortable in the hand and has a sturdy, durable hinge.

Gin: This grain-based liquor gets its distinctive flavour from juniper berries and is often enjoyed as an ingredient in cocktails. The most popular of these beverages is the dry martini, but hundreds of gin mixed drinks exist, from gin and tonic to the Negroni (Campari, sweet vermouth, and gin) and the gimlet (lime juice, sugar, and gin).

Ginger preserves: This intensely flavoured sweet and spicy spread is a traditional accompaniment to scones and other breads. It can also be served alongside meat and poultry or used in a glaze.

Ginger, crystallised: Ginger that has been crystallised in sugar syrup and then coated with granulated sugar adds sweet-pungent flavour to any dish it's used in. Ginger lovers enjoy it as a snack or garnish.

Gratin dish: Gratins, a French specialty, are baked dishes quickly recognisable by their crisp browned tops, often sprinkled with cheese or bread crumbs to give extra texture and flavour. Traditional gratin dishes are wide and just deep enough to allow a delicious contrast between the bubbling brown surface and the tender layers beneath.

Grenache: This red wine grape widely cultivated in the south of France and in Spain (where it's known as Garnacha) is both blended with other types of grapes and used to make single-varietal wines, which tend to be very fruity and soft on the palate and are best drunk fairly young.

Grüner Veltliner: Pronounced "*grewn*-uh *velt*-lin-uh," this Austrian white wine is growing in popularity. Its clean, fresh, citrusy-floral flavour pairs well with a wide range of foods and cuisines, including Asian.

Highball glass: The shape of this tall, narrow glass helps keep drinks from going flat, so it's most often used for fizzy cocktails containing tonic or soda water. It typically holds 250ml-375ml (8–12 fl oz) of liquid.

Hoisin sauce: This sweet, tangy, reddish brown Chinese sauce is made from fermented soybeans, vinegar, sugar, garlic, and spices. It can be thick and creamy or thin enough to pour. The versatile sauce is used to flavour meat dishes, is added to dipping sauces, and is offered at the table as a condiment. It should be used judiciously, as its strong flavour can easily overpower most foods. Sold in jars, it will keep indefinitely stored in the refrigerator.

Jigger: This measuring tool, often in the form of a small metal cup with flared sides, is used to measure ingredients when making cocktails. Two-sided jiggers have 2 cups, one usually measuring 3 Tbsp (the jigger) and the other 2 Tbsp (the pony), so verify how large yours is before you use it. A shot glass with measuring lines on it can be used instead.

Lemongrass: This long, slender, fibrous lemon-scented grass is native to Asia. The coarse, paper-dry upper portion is cut off and discarded, and the bulbous base, usually 7.5–10 cm (3–4 in) long, is either pounded, thinly sliced, or minced to release its fragrance. Each minced stalk will give you about 1 Tbsp lemongrass. When cut crosswise, a fine series of concentric rings is revealed. If fresh lemongrass is not available, substitute 1 Tbsp slivered lemon balm or chopped lemon zest. Keep lemongrass for up to 2 weeks in a refrigerator crisper.

Limoncello: This sweet liqueur from southern Italy is made by infusing grain spirits with lemon peel. Traditionally drunk after dinner as a digestive, it's increasingly popular as a component in cocktails.

Martini glass: Also called a cocktail glass, this long-stemmed glass with a cone-shaped bowl is used for many classic cocktails, such as martinis and Manhattans, which are served up (shaken or stirred with ice and then strained). An average martini glass holds about 125ml (4 fl oz) of liquid.

Muddler: This long wooden stick with a blunt, often ridged end, is used to crush herbs, fruit, and sugar cubes when making cocktails. If you don't have a muddler, you can use a long-handled wooden spoon instead.

Muscat, orange: Though the origins of this little-known grape varietal are disputed, some believe it came from the south of France, around the town of Orange. Orange Muscat is enjoying a resurgence in popularity as vintners are turning it into a highly perfumed sweet wine with aromas of orange blossom, peaches, and honey, served as an aperitif or as an accompaniment to dessert.

Mustard, dry: Available in the spice section of grocery stores, dry mustard is the ground seeds of the mustard plant. This yellow powder can be mixed with water, vinegar, or other liquid to make mustard, used in spice rubs, or used to season many types of dishes.

Nutmeg: The large, oval, brown seed of a soft fruit, nutmeg has a warm, sweet, spicy flavour. Whole nutmeg keeps its flavour much longer than ground nutmeg. Always grate nutmeg just before using. Use the finest rasps on a box grater, or a specialised nutmeg grater.

Old Bay seasoning: One of the distinctive flavours of mid-Atlantic cooking, this zesty spice blend finds its way into many dishes, especially shellfish recipes. The exact proportions are proprietary, but the mixture includes celery salt, mustard, red pepper flakes, black pepper, bay leaf, cloves, allspice, ginger, mace, cardamom, cassia (a spice similar to cinnamon), and paprika.

Old-fashioned glass: This short, squat, straight-sided glass is used for small mixed drinks and shots of liquor served on ice. It typically holds 125-250ml (4 to 8 fl oz) of liquid.

Orange flower water: Made by distilling the blossoms of the bitter orange, this aromatic water is used in small amounts to flavour cocktails, desserts, and other dishes.

Oranges, blood: Available in many markets winter through spring, blood oranges have ruby-coloured flesh with a raspberry-tinged fragrance and flavour. The amount of red on the skin often indicates the depth of colour inside.

Parmesan cheese: A firm, aged, salty cheese made from cow's milk. True Parmesan, produced in the Emilia-Romagna region of Italy, is known by the trademarked name Parmigiano-Reggiano. Look for the name stamped in a pattern on the rind. To ensure freshness, purchase the cheese in wedges and grate or shave it only as needed for use in a recipe. Store Parmesan cheese wrapped in waxed paper or plastic in the refrigerator for up to 3 weeks.

Pastry blender: This tool, used to cut butter and other fats into flour for flaky pastry crusts, consists of a sturdy handle anchoring a row of wires or blades. The wires cut the butter into smaller and smaller pieces until it resembles small peas or coarse meal.

Pepper, white: Made from peppercorns that have had their skins removed and berries dried, white pepper is often less aromatic and milder in flavour than black pepper. It is favoured in the preparation of light-coloured sauces when cooks want to avoid flecks of black pepper in the final dish.

Peppercorns, coarsely cracked: You can buy cracked peppercorns, or put whole peppercorns in a heavy-duty zipped plastic bag and crush them gently with a frying pan.

Pinot Grigio: An Italian grape varietal that is also grown in California and Oregon, Pinot Grigio (or Pinot Gris) is used to make delicate, light-bodied white wines that tend to be crisp and acidic. The Italians like to pair this wine with seafood and light pasta dishes.

Pinot Noir: *See* Burgundy.

Pony: *See* Jigger.

Port, tawny: Port is available in three types: sweet ruby Port, as red as its name; amber-coloured, drier tawny Port, good for both drinking and cooking; and the most expensive, vintage Port, which is rich and complex, and can be aged for decades.

Retsina: This Greek white wine with a resinous flavour reputedly originated in the ancient practice of storing wine in vessels sealed with pine resin. Though its pungent aroma means it's an acquired taste for some, others find it the perfect accompaniment to strongly flavoured Greek and other Mediterranean food.

Riesling: This crisp, floral white wine, native to Germany, has a flavour that brings to mind summer tree fruits, flint, or even a hint of smoke. Riesling ranges from quite sweet to fairly dry. Slightly sweet Riesling, called "off-dry," is made not only in Germany, but also in California, Australia, and New Zealand.

Rocket: The leaves of this dark green plant, resemble deeply notched, elongated oak leaves. They have a nutty, tangy, and slightly peppery flavour. The larger leaves may have a coarser texture and more pungent flavour than small ones.

Rum: A spirit that originated in the Caribbean, rum is distilled from sugarcane juice or molasses. This slightly sweet liquor is especially well suited for mixed drinks and desserts. Rums flavoured with orange, vanilla, and tropical flavours such as banana and coconut are available at most grocery and liquor stores.

Sake: Although it is sometimes called "rice wine," this Japanese beverage is actually brewed somewhat like beer. It is served both cold and hot, though higher-quality sakes are served cold so as not to destroy their delicate flavours by heating.

Salt, sea: Created by natural evaporation, sea salt is available in coarse or fine grains that are shaped like hollow, flaky pyramids. Due to its shape, it adheres better to foods and dissolves more quickly than table salt. Sea salt from France (such as the prized Fleur du Sel), England, and the United States is available in well-stocked supermarkets.

Scant: A scant measurement is just slightly less than the full amount.

Sesame oil: A dark amber-coloured oil pressed from toasted white sesame seeds, Asian sesame oil has a rich, distinctive nutty aroma and taste. Like a good extra-virgin oil, sesame oil does not heat well. It's best used in small amounts as a flavouring agent for marinades and dressings or for soups and braised or stir-fried dishes during the final minutes of cooking. Don't confuse Asian sesame oil with the clear-pressed sesame seed oil sold in natural-foods stores, which is made from raw white sesame seeds.

Sesame seeds: These tiny, flat seeds are available in brown, red, and black varieties, but the most common are white sesame seeds. They add a nutty flavour to any food, especially when toasted, and are often sprinkled over savoury dishes as a garnish.

Skewers, bamboo: Bamboo skewers should be soaked to keep them from burning. Soak them in water for about 30 minutes, then drain and thread the food to be grilled onto the skewers, covering as much of each skewer as possible. You can also wrap any exposed skewer in aluminum foil. If you want to forgo soaking, look for metal skewers.

Soba noodles: Thin, brownish grey soba noodles, made from buckwheat, are enormously popular in Japan. These are available fresh and dried in Japanese markets; the dried variety may also be found in the ethnic aisle of well-stocked supermarkets.

Stick blender: Also called an immersion or a handheld blender, this tool has a motor in the handle and rotating blade at the other end. Used to purée soups and sauces without removing them from their mixing bowl or pot, they are particularly useful for puréeing hot foods. Be sure to submerge the blade completely to prevent spattering.

Sugar, superfine: When finely ground, granulated sugar becomes superfine sugar, also known as castor or caster sugar. Because it dissolves rapidly, it is preferred for cold recipes such as mixed drinks (it is also sold as bar sugar) and for delicate mixtures such as beaten egg whites.

Syrah: Known as shiraz in Australia, syrah in the United States and in France, this grape is used to produce an intensely flavoured, medium- to full-bodied red wine. Though it can vary considerably in style, shiraz or syrah tends to have an aroma of blackberries or black cherry and pepper. Spicy and tannic when young, it often develops a more earthy or leathery flavour when aged. It pairs well with grilled meats, sausages, and peppery stews.

Tequila: Tequila is made from the fermented and distilled juice of the blue agave (a succulent plant). There are three styles: sharp-tasting blanco, also known as silver or white tequila, aged in steel for 60 days; reposado, aged in wooden casks for 60 days; and the more refined añejo, which spends at least a year in wooden casks. Note that gold tequila is simply a blanco that has been tinted brown.

Triple Sec: Traditionally made using the dried peel of oranges, this colorless orange-flavoured liqueur is used to sweeten a variety of cocktails, such as margaritas and Long Island iced teas.

Vanilla: Vanilla extract, also known as vanilla essence, is made by chopping vanilla beans and soaking them in a mixture of alcohol and water, then aging the solution. Look for pure extracts made from beans from Tahiti (more subtle flavour) or Madagascar (stronger flavour). Imitation vanilla has a thin, chemical flavour that dissipates quickly, and should be avoided. Always let hot foods cool off for a few minutes before adding vanilla extract; otherwise, the heat will evaporate the alcohol, and along with it some of the vanilla flavour.

Vermouth: A fortified wine flavoured with various spices, herbs, and fruits, vermouth is available in two basic styles: sweet (also known as Italian or red) and dry. Dry vermouth, an ingredient in the classic martini, is also used in cooking, and is especially good when making a pan sauce.

Viognier: Wines made from the Viognier grape—which has traditionally been grown in France's Rhône region but is now more common in California and Australia—have a deep golden colour and a complex aroma of tropical fruit, apricots, and flowers. Viogniers tend to have low acid and be fairly dry, and are a good match for spicy Chinese or Thai food, boldly flavoured seafood dishes, pork, and chicken. Pronounced "*vee*-oh-nyeh."

Vodka: Originally made from potatoes, today vodka is usually made from grain. Unaged and clear, vodka has little taste and so may be blended with a variety of other liquids. It is also sold in a wide variety of flavoured forms, such as vanilla, raspberry, and pepper.

Vouvray: Wines from this French region, made from the Chenin Blanc grape, feature a range of styles, from dry and crisp to lush, fruity, and sweet. Pronounced "voo-*vray*."

Watermelon rind, pickled: Popular in the American South as well as parts of Asia, pickled watermelon rind is made by soaking the rind in a brine solution and boiling it in a sugar and vinegar syrup. If you don't want to make your own, it's available in jars at specialty stores and some well-stocked supermarkets.

Whisk(e)y: Including bourbon, rye, Scotch, Canadian, and Irish, whiskeys are all made from grain. Scotch whisky (correctly spelled without an *e*), which includes unblended "single" malt whiskies, is often simply called Scotch. Bourbon, which takes its name from a county in Kentucky, is made from fermented grain, usually corn. Most Canadian whiskies are blended whiskies made primarily from corn and rye, and are lighter in style than other types of the spirit.

Worcestershire sauce: A traditional English condiment, Worcestershire sauce is an intensely flavourful and savoury blend of varied ingredients, including molasses, soy sauce, garlic, onion, and anchovies. Popular in marinades for grilled food, it can also be passed at the table.

Yoghurt, Greek: Usually made from whole milk, thick Greek-style yoghurt doesn't need to be drained before using it in cooking. Look for it in Greek specialty stores, the dairy section of natural-foods stores, and some supermarkets.

Za'atar: This aromatic blend of spices popular in the Middle East and North Africa is used to season meats and vegetables and is mixed with olive oil to make a dip. Though the recipe varies, it contains primarily ground sumac, a spice, and toasted sesame seeds, along with thyme and salt. Za'atar can be found in well-stocked supermarkets and Middle Eastern grocery stores.

Zinfandel, old-vine: Although long considered a California native, the Zinfandel grape in fact has the same DNA as Italian primitivo. This full-bodied red wine gives off an aroma of blackberries and spice, and its substantial structure and robust flavour make it a great complement to hearty foods like grilled or broiled steaks and chops. Old-vine Zinfandel, which is thought by many to have an earthier quality and more complex flavour, is made from vines planted roughly fifty to more than a hundred years ago.

Index

Bonnier Books,
Appledram Barns, Birdham Road,
Chichester PO20 7EQ
www.bonnierbooks.co.uk

First published in the UK by Bonnier Books, 2008

WELDON OWEN INC.

Chief Executive Officer, Weldon Owen Group John Owen
President and Chief Executive Officer, Weldon Owen Inc. Terry Newell
Chief Financial Officer Simon Fraser
Vice President, International Sales Stuart Laurence
Vice President, Sales & New Business Development Amy Kaneko
Vice President & Creative Director Gaye Allen
Vice President & Publisher Hannah Rahill
Associate Publisher Amy Marr
Executive Editor Sarah Putman Clegg
Senior Art Director Emma Boys
Designer Diana Heom
Production Director Chris Hemesath
Production Manager Michelle Duggan
Colour Manager Teri Bell
Production and Reprint Coordinator Todd Rechner
Photo Coordinator Meghan Hildebrand

BRIDE & GROOM ENTERTAINING COOKBOOK

Conceived and produced by Weldon Owen Inc.
814 Montgomery Street, San Francisco, CA 94133
Telephone: 415 291 0100 Fax: 415 291 8841

In collaboration with Williams-Sonoma, Inc.
3250 Van Ness Avenue, San Francisco, CA 94109

A WELDON OWEN PRODUCTION

Set in Myriad MM, Perpetua, Marydale

Colour separations by Embassy Graphics.
Printed and bound in China by Midas Printing Limited.

ISBN-13: 978-1-905825-51-6

ACKNOWLEDGEMENTS

Weldon Owen wishes to thank the following people for their generous support in producing this book:

Photographer David Matheson
Photo Assistant Matt Stevens
Food Stylist Alison Attenborough
Assistant Food Stylist Lillian Kang
Prop Stylist Bergren Rameson
Assistant Prop Stylist Taylor McCarthy
Copy Editor Carrie Bradley
Consulting Editor Sharon Silva
Proofreader Sharron Wood
Indexer Ken DellaPenta

Models and Homeowners
Herman Chan
Aaron Fagerstrom
Jana Ireton
Erin Kelly
Claudia Ossa
Cynthia Wright and David Easton
Rod Rougelot

Additional photography:
page 16 *(upper left)* by Joe Keller